Creating Online Courses and Orientations

Creating Online Courses and Orientations

A Survival Guide

Pamela S. Bacon and David Bagwell Jr.

LIBRARIES
UNLIMITED
A Member of the Greenwood Publishing Group

Westport, Connecticut • London

Library of Congress Cataloging-in-Publication Data

Bacon, Pamela S., 1964-
   Creating online courses and orientations : a survival guide / by
Pamela S. Bacon and David Bagwell Jr.
   p. cm.
   Includes bibliographical references and index.
   ISBN 1-59158-289-X (pbk. : alk. paper)
   1. Education, Secondary—Computer network resources. 2. Media
programs (Education) 3. Teaching—Aids and devices. I. Bagwell,
David. II. Title.
   LB1044.87.B33 2005
   373.133'4—dc22 2005020656

British Library Cataloguing in Publication Data is available.

Library of Congress Catalog Card Number: 2005020656
ISBN: 1-59158-289-X

First published in 2005

Libraries Unlimited, 88 Post Road West, Westport, CT 06881
A Member of the Greenwood Publishing Group, Inc.
www.lu.com

Printed in the United States of America

The paper used in this book complies with the
Permanent Paper Standard issued by the National
Information Standards Organization (Z39.48–1984).

10 9 8 7 6 5 4 3 2 1

*To my survival tools: My husband, Scott, my son, James,
and especially my twin sister, Tammy.*

P. Bacon

*As this is my first book, I want to dedicate it to my wife, Marti,
and my four children: Jessica, Valarie, Daniel, and Matthew.*

D. Bagwell

CONTENTS

Survival Guide to Online Courses

"Capture the Giant:"
Online Research Skills Unit

Appendixes

ACKNOWLEDGMENTS

While Dave wanted to thank me for including him in this book project, I'd like to also thank him for his valuable coauthoring skills—especially formatting! He was truly a survival tool for me! We would like to acknowledge the following people for their assistance in this project:

Kaaren Baumgartner, whose offhand comment sparked a "Giant" project!

Valarie Bagwell, whose literary skills and expertise are truly appreciated.

Mrs. Fulford and her business technology students for assistance with word processing.

Kelly Rich, Rachel Helbling, and Libby Lawrie—three unsinkable lifesavers!

Krista Hensley, Gary Moorman, and Jenny Aykroyd—and their awesome students for their "giant" participation in the pilot project.

BDHS students Jason Hardin and Montana Milnes for their assistance whenever and wherever needed.

CONTRIBUTORS

Katie Gallagher
  5225 East 56th Street
  Indianapolis, IN 46226

Rachel Helbling
  3350 W. Baltimore Woodlands N.
  Monrovia, IN 46157

Elizabeth J. Oyer (Ph.D.)
  Evaluation Solutions
  Carmel, IN 46032

Kelly Rich
  1830 Sonesta Lane
  Indianapolis, IN 46217

Student Contributors

Jeremy M. Barker
  Ben Davis High School Student

Kelsey E. Breece
  Ben Davis High School Student

Matt Carter
  Ben Davis High School Student

Joshua A. Coe
  Ben Davis High School Student

Jacob DeWitt
  Ben Davis High School Student

Marlowe C. Haddix
  Ben Davis High School Student

Benjamin M. Jarvis
  Ben Davis High School Student

Mary C. Jenkins
  Ben Davis High School Student

Kristin Lucero
  Ben Davis High School Student

Benjamin E. Stevens
  Ben Davis High School Student

James David Thomas II
  Ben Davis High School Student

Allison M. Tyler
  Ben Davis High School Student

Blake Vanderbush
  Ben Davis High School Student

INTRODUCTION

When my former colleague, Kaaren Baumgartner, made an offhand comment about going online with our orientation program, a seed was planted in my mind. That seed has now developed into a full-grown beanstalk—in the form of an online research skills unit, known as "Capture the Giant!" In this online unit, students set off to prevent the giant (our school mascot) from capturing valuable information skills and doing away with them forever.

I must admit that the thought of creating an online course was somewhat daunting at first. That's where Dave, my coauthor, came in. As technology supervisor and headmaster of the Indiana Online Academy (our online school), I knew Dave could be a "giant" help to me. Not only does Dave have the "techie" background (whereas I'm the "bookie"), he also teaches an online class at a local college. In the creation of my course, I sat down with Dave to discuss some advantages of going online. At that time, the time needed to create such a project seemed insurmountable, but after talking with Dave, I decided to start climbing!

You may be asking, "Why go online?"

- **Increased Access**—"The primary reason for creating an online course is to provide access" (Klemm 2001, 1). Because online learning can take place anywhere and any time, this reason alone often accounts for the ever-increasing popularity of distance learning. Space and time barriers are instantly removed, allowing greater access for students with jobs, extracurricular activities, and busy schedules. Students have virtual access to up-to-date content and learning 24 hours a day!

- **Limited Staffing**—Thanks to budget cuts, when Kaaren retired, our administration was not able to fill her position. Even with limited staffing, the online unit allows me to reach all students and teach valuable research and library-related lessons—something I never could have done using the traditional "face to face" approach.

- **Increased Student Enrollment**—Our school, the largest three-year high school in the state of Indiana, has almost 3,000 students—and is still growing! The online course allows me to have some type of interaction, albeit not personal, with each and every student.

- **Increased Staff**—As you would expect, a larger student population leads to a larger teacher population. With almost 30 full-time English teachers, there is no way that I could physically meet the orientation needs of every class. Even if every English teacher brought his or her students to the media center for a week-long orientation and research unit, I'd never survive—and we'd have to increase the school year to do it!

- **Increased Student Achievement**—If your school is like ours, the bottom line is student achievement. Since I've started the online orientation, I have seen a definite rise in student achievement. With our data-driven educational state, I now have data to prove that the program works—and works well.

- **Increased Number of Collaborative Units**—By taking advantage of the online content, I'm no longer spending all of my time teaching introductory library skills; my time is now freed up to work collaboratively with teachers. I can now co-plan, co-teach, and even co-grade special units.

- **Increased Availability**—Once an online unit has been created, other schools can use and even modify the content or material. Collaboration can take place, allowing more than one school to take advantage of already-created online instructional units and teach students as they move through the school system. Teachers in our Freshman Center will be able to coordinate lessons by knowing in advance what content and skills students will learn when they become sophomores. In addition, eight of our elementary schools can collaborate to create online content that they can all use, as opposed to creating eight separate lessons and duplicating efforts.

- **Increased Awareness**—Since I've started this unit, I now have administrators, teachers, parents, and students who understand that library standards and critical information skills exist and really matter. In addition, all parties involved now see me in a teaching role, and there is more support as a result.

- **Increased Motivation**—Like it or not, students love to use computers! Students who would normally have behavior problems now are more actively involved in their learning. Even though some of the same information is taught, learning online is more user-friendly and interesting to students.

Now that you know the many advantages to developing an online course, you're probably ready to get started right away. To help you, part I of the book is the SURVIVAL GUIDE, broken down into manageable steps for you to follow to create your own online course. Throughout part I you'll see

- Survival Strategies (advice from teachers—or students—in the trenches!),

- Survival Tips (practical advice),

- Survival Sources (Internet resources),

- Survival Tools (ready-to-use reproducibles), and

- Survival Advice/Bagwell's Blogs

Part II contains my online research skills unit, "Capture the Giant." You can modify the unit to suit your own needs. Finally, part III contains appendixes for your convenience and review.

Although not mandatory, the appendixes include nuts and bolts to assist you in the implementation of your own online course.

Although all Web site URLs were accurate and active at the time of publication, URLs change frequently and may no longer be current.

Don't hesitate to contact us if you need help keeping afloat once you get started!

Part I

SURVIVAL GUIDE TO ONLINE COURSES

Survival Tools Guide

Survival Tool 1a: The Goals Grid—The Goals Grid is a useful tool to help you achieve goal clarity by looking at a goal from four different perspectives. "Goal" for it!

Survival Tool 1b: Objectives Rubric—For this tool, "X" marks the spot and gives you an "objective" way to evaluate your course objectives.

Survival Tool 2: Teaching Online: Problems and Solutions T-Chart—Dave understands your problems to a "T" and offers solutions.

Survival Tool 3: Just the FAQs!—You've got questions? We've got answers!

Survival Tool 4: Notesheet for Evaluating Online Courses—This handy tool, in checklist format, is a cheat sheet for evaluating online courses.

Survival Tool 5: Lesson Planning Sheet—Got a plan? Now you do! This simple form walks you through your lesson plan—whether traditional or online.

Survival Tool 6a: Giant PowerPoint Presentation—A "giant" help to introduce students to the online unit.

Survival Tool 6b: Ticket for the Test—This tool is "just the ticket" you need to give to your students when they master the ten Giant steps.

Survival Tool 7a: Differentiation Checklist—Get the number on your DI needs!

Survival Tool 7b: Differentiation Questions—You'll have all the answers you need to differentiate instruction when you go through these five questions.

Survival Tool 7c: Differentiating Instruction Strategies—This step-by-step (literally!) strategy tool helps you easily meet the needs of your low-, average-, and high-level students.

Survival Tool 8: Feedback Form—Students will "eat up" the chance to give you feedback on the unit—and you'll be "full" of information!

Survival Tool 9a: Grading Sheet—This rubric makes the grade—by giving you a handy way to score those units.

Survival Tool 9b: Grading Checklist—"Check" out this tool when you get ready to grade the online units.

Survival Tool 10: Standards Chart—You'll be above board standards (school board, that is) when you use this tool to show how each of the ten Giant steps meet Big6 Skills, Information Literacy Standards, and the language arts curriculum.

Survival Tool 11a: Research Unit Reminders—Print out this tool and post it in classrooms to remind students (and you!) when the final project is due.

Survival Tool 11b: Discussion Boards—This tool is a "don't!" *Don't* do what I did—make sure you put guidelines in place for student use of discussion boards. *Do* monitor!

Survival Tool 12: Data Decisions—"Count" on success when you tally up the number of classes that have completed the online unit.

Survival Tool 13a: Online Course Evaluation—Of "course" you'll want to evaluate at the end of the orientation!

Survival Tool 13b: Online Instructor Evaluation—Did YOU make the grade? Get an "A" for adaptive when you use relevant feedback to improve instruction.

Survival Sources: A Sneak Peek

Chapter 1: Set Objectives and Goals—Getting Started
http://www.personal.psu.edu/staff/b/x/bxb11/Objectives/

> This site gives specific directions and provides color-coded examples for writing goals and objectives.

Chapter 2: Understand the Barriers
http://mnscsc.org/Socrates/elearning/downloads/probs_opps_ollchecklst.pdf

> This site provides a survey listing the advantages and challenges to online learning. It would be a handy survey for assessing the teachers in your building to determine their readiness level regarding utilizing online courses with students.

Chapter 3: Read, Research, and Resources
http://www.blackboard.com

> Blackboard's starting point for online support.

http://stylusinc.com/online_course/tutorial/process.htm

> A step-by-step guide to developing online courses.

http://ts.mivu.org/default.asp?show=article&id=861

> Another useful tool for creating online courses.

http://www.pitt.edu/~poole/onlinelearning.html#designingOLactivities

> The research and resources on this site are endless. Caution: Don't jump in if you are in a hurry!

Chapter 4: View Other Courses to Determine Format (Virtual Visits)
http://www.nwrel.org/mentoring/elearning.html

> The National Mentoring Center is in the process of studying online learning formats and is dedicated to helping to improve the quality of online courses. Check out this site often for the latest research and findings.

Chapter 5: Instruction—Plan Activities, Develop Lessons, Decide on Course Content
http://www.eduref.org/cgi-bin/lessons.cgi/Language_Arts

> The Educator's Resource Guide includes a wealth of lesson plans and activities to view for course content ideas.

Chapter 6: Visit Classrooms and Pilot Program (Promotion)
http://www.keele.ac.uk/depts/aa/landt/links/POTguidelines.htm

> This site includes some important points for peer observations—important guidelines when visiting other teachers' classrooms and/or reviewing a peer's program.

Chapter 7: Adapt Unit to Meet Individual Needs—Differentiate!
http://www.support4learning.org.uk/education/lstyles.htm

> This site provides countless resources and information on differentiation strategies, learning styles, and multiple intelligences.

Chapter 8: Listen to Feedback
http://www.yale.edu/ynhti/pubs/A14/polio.html

> This site concurs that student feedback is all too often left out of evaluation. It also clarifies the roles of various stakeholders in the online learning game.

Chapter 9: Grading—Get a Plan!
http://www.teachervision.fen.com/page/26773.html

> "Is this for a grade?" If this sounds familiar, check out this source, which provides specific rubric examples for a variety of library and literacy lessons for K–12 student assessments—a perfect tool to assist teachers with grading everything from projects to writing samples.

Chapter 10: Unwrap the Standards
http://www.awesomelibrary.org/Office/Teacher/Standards/Standards.html

> The Awesome Library site includes valuable information from the U.S. Department of Education outlining the process for developing and implementing standards-based units.

Chapter 11: Implement Online Course
http://ncsdweb.ncsd.k12.wy.us/dherman/Lesley/week2/lesson/lesson_rubric.html

> This site provides an example of a rubric that could be utilized for teacher self-reflection *after* lesson implementation. It could also easily be used *before* the lesson to ensure that critical components, like library standards and course content, are covered.

Chapter 12: Data, Data, Data!
http://depts.washington.edu/oeaias/

> The IAS (Instructional Assessment System) Online site includes a sample data collection form and a sample report, which could be modified and used for your own data collection. View a demo and, if funds are available, find out rates for IAS to create a custom database for your data collection needs. This is a data collection site you can count on to make data decisions a little easier.

Chapter 13: Evaluate
http://www.remc11.k12.mi.us/bcisd/classres/restch.htm

> This site is invaluable after you have evaluated your course and are ready to refine or research areas for improvement or extension.

Chapter 1

SET OBJECTIVES AND GOALS—GETTING STARTED

Survival Strategy

This experiment of library knowledge has been quite helpful to me. Previously, I had little or no knowledge of how a library worked. Now, I have the confidence that will help me understand how to find books and other materials.—J. D. Thomas II, BDHS Sophomore **(Goal Met! pb)**

This first step is one of the hardest, but most important, steps you will take. Quite simply, what do you want the students to know? You must decide at this point what you ultimately want the students to know or accomplish when they have completed the course or unit. A basic goal for this project might be: "Students will learn valuable research skills."

Often, however, the goal is based on a need—something students don't presently know that you would like them to know. In my case, for example, I recognized the need for students to be able to evaluate Web sites. Our students were gaining competency and skill in Internet searching, but they were not evaluating what they were finding. Instead, they were taking all sites at face value, believing all Web sites were created equal! To rectify this, I set the following goal: "All sophomores at Ben Davis High School will learn specific criteria with which to evaluate a Web site." (See how the goal is getting more specific?)

Finally, based on need, teachers can develop more specific instructional goals. Learning goals are mastered through accomplishing certain objectives. An example of an instructional goal and objectives for this project might be: "Each student will complete a ten-step online orientation and reach 80 percent mastery on the final assessment."

Just having a basic understanding of your goals and objectives can help you plan your course by starting with the end (what you want students to ultimately accomplish) in mind. Keep in mind that goals and objectives should be measurable and should answer the following questions.

Survival Tips

- What are the educational goals and objectives?

- How will these goals be accomplished?

- Which goals might not be accomplished, and what accommodations can be made for them?

- When students meet goals, are they also meeting standards?

- What information or skills do students need to be able to successfully meet these goals and objectives?

- How much time is needed for goals and objectives to be met?

- How much will this course cost to create? Where will the money come from?

Another tool to help you as you set goals for your online unit is "The Goals Grid," developed by Fred Nickols (Survival Tool 1a). Nickols (with a little help from his colleagues) developed the tool to help users achieve goal clarity. By prompting us to think about goals and objectives in an organized, structured fashion, goals and objectives become better. The Goals Grid helps answer some basic questions:

1. What are we really up to here?

2. Do we have all the bases covered?

3. What are we overlooking?

4. Have we adequately thought this thing through?

5. How do our various goals and objectives relate to one another?

6. What do the patterns tell us about our willingness to risk and to change?

7. Are we in conflict with others?

The Goals Grid is simply a framework for thinking about and asking tough questions about goals and objectives. Do all of your goals fall into Quadrant II (Avoid) or Quadrant IV (Eliminate)? If so, perhaps you're focusing too much on the negative. On the other hand, if no goals involve these quadrants, perhaps you're not being open-minded or realistic. Finding a balance is key.

Let's use a realistic example from above and work through The Goals Grid together. For example, let's say our goal is: "Each student will complete a ten-step online orientation and reach 80 percent mastery on the final assessment."

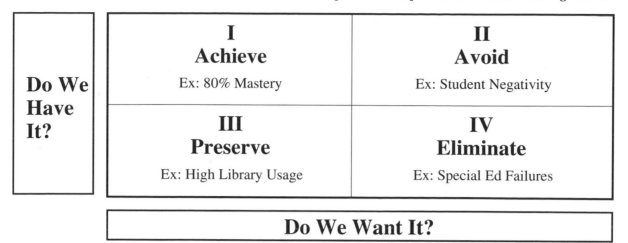

The Goals Grid. Created by Fred Nickols

Notes: As you can see, working through "The Goals Grid" can be extremely helpful in making your goals and objectives clear and focused. If possible, work through your goals with a colleague to ensure you're staying objective—and seeing things from all different perspectives. Grid-locked? Take a break and come back to it when you're fresh!

Depending on what you find in your grid exercise, you may want to write other goals based on your findings. For example, I admitted that maintaining high library usage was a priority, yet this unit is online and independent, requiring possibly fewer media center visits. How might I address this goal, yet still meet my objectives?

- **Quadrant I: Achieve**

   Write in what you want to achieve (from goal above). Example: 80% Mastery
   Next, ask yourself:
   > Do we have it? Not yet!
   > Do we want it? Yes!

- **Quadrant II: Avoid**

   Write in what you want to avoid. Example: Student Negativity
   Next, ask yourself:
   > Do we have it? No!
   > Do we want it? No!

- **Quadrant III: Preserve**

   Write in what you have now that you want to preserve. Example: Library Usage
   Next, ask yourself:
   > Do we have it? Yes!
   > Do we want it? Yes!

- **Quadrant IV: Eliminate**

    Write in what you want to eliminate. Example: Special Ed Failures

    Do we have it? Yes!

    Do we want it? No!

Author Note: This was a real eye opener for me. When I wrote the goal, I felt confident about it. After using The Goals Grid, I started wondering if my original goal shouldn't be revised to include adaptations for special needs students. Thus, I changed my original goal from ten "Giant Steps" to seven to ten "Giant Steps" (based on individual needs).

Finally, once you've used the Goals Grid to determine your objectives, "see" if your objective floats by using the Objectives Rubic (Survival Tool 1b).

Set Objectives and Goals

> Katie Gallagher has taught an economics course for the Indiana Online Academy (IOA) since 2001. She also teaches online psychology for Cathedral High School in Indianapolis. During a recent presentation, she focused on the critical need to set specific goals and objectives before creating online content. Perhaps because of her intentional goal setting, Katie's courses are excellent examples of interactivity and reflect the importance of using interactive tools such as e-mail, chat, and message boards for students to communicate with each other—and her!
>
> "Organization and ease of navigation is critical. Courses or lessons should be created with the end in mind and focus on standards" (Katie Gallagher—Angel Users Conference—May 14, 2004, Creating Effective Online Classes).

Survival Source 1

http://www.personal.psu.edu/staff/b/x/bxb11/Objectives/

This site gives specific directions and provides color-coded examples for writing goals and objectives.

The Goals Grid
Created by Fred Nickols

NO	**I** **Achieve** Goal:	**II** **Avoid** Goal:
Do We Have It?		
	III **Preserve** Goal:	**IV** **Eliminate** Goal:
YES		

Do We Want It?

YES   NO

Survival Tool 1a. The Goals Grid

This Survival Tool was adapted with permission from the author, Fred Nickols. To read "The Goals Grid: A Tool for Clarifying Goals and Objectives" article in its entirety, go to http://home.att.net/~nickols/goals_grid.htm.

What Counts?	Competent Work	Common Mistake	Needs to Be Revised	Missed the Point
The objectives are measurable.	The objectives are measurable and include specific information about what the student will be able to do (e.g. how well, how many, to what degree).	The objectives are too general and don't include specific information on what the student will be able to do (e.g. how well, how many, to what degree).	The objectives are not measurable. The objectives don't describe what the student will be able to do.	The objectives are not universally measurable and do not include what the student will be able to do.
Objectives require high levels of cognition.	The objectives reflect high levels of cognition according to Bloom's Taxonomy	All the objectives require low levels of cognition, such as "demonstrates understanding" or "identifies."	The objectives should include at least one of the verbs in the levels 3–6 in Bloom's Taxonomy.	The objectives don't use verbs to describe what the student will be able to do.
The learning objectives should be achievable.	The objectives listed are realistic given the time and level of the target audience.	There are too many objectives.	The objectives are too difficult.	The objectives don't use verbs.
Are the goals of interest to the learner?	The learning objectives are of interest to the learner.	The learning objectives don't make the intrinsic and external motivation clear to the learner.	The learner can't understand the learning objectives.	The learner doesn't want to complete tasks in the learning objectives.

Survival Tool 1b. Objectives Rubric

By Valerie Landau, Assistant Professor of Multimedia, California State University. Reprinted with permission from *Developing an Effective Online Course* by Valerie Landau (Seaside, CA: Round World Media, 2001).

Chapter 2

UNDERSTAND THE BARRIERS

Survival Strategy

It is difficult to complete the Giant Steps, being in the media center only once a week!—Marlowe Haddix, BDHS Senior **(Obviously, time is always a barrier! pb)**

Of all the things I've never done, this was the most productive! —Jacob DeWitt, BDHS Senior **(Gifted students can sometimes be a barrier! Jacob found creative ways around the system NOT to participate—and made the book anyway! Go figure! pb)**

Even given all of the advantages to online learning, there are, admittedly, some barriers and hurdles to overcome. By taking a proactive stance, however, the "Three T" barriers (time, technology, and teaching) can easily be overcome. See Survival Tool 2 for other barriers.

Time

One of the biggest barriers to face is the amount of time needed to create an online course. Creating an online course is one of the biggest challenges that I have taken on—but also one of the most worthwhile. Keep in mind that, once the course is created, you will be able to save time in the future. You only have to create the course once. While you may (and should) make continual revisions to the course, the biggest chunk of time is in the creation, not the revision. If you take the time now to create a quality, standards-based course, you'll be able to use it for years to come.

Technology

Other than course content, another huge time-taker involves technology. Learning new technology, deciding on course delivery options, and working with your school's technology team to get the course up and running can be extremely time-consuming. "Despite these challenges, the benefits of an online course outweigh the time consumed creating it" (Klemm 2001, 2).

Another technology issue is the course upkeep. To be effective, it is critical to keep the course content and site updated. Failing to update the course results in outdated, old (and boring) information—just the opposite of what you intended when you started the process! Finding a competent Web designer will be invaluable to you as you go through this process. Remember, you don't have to have the "techie" skills to create and update the site, but you do have to be able to find the help you need!

The last barrier to online success lies ironically in the medium itself. In today's world, there are several issues to consider when using technology as a teaching tool.

Teaching with Technology Issues

In an online course, students are more exposed to

- Internet safety (protecting students from sharing personal information with strangers),

- copyright violations (properly citing Internet sources), and

- classroom management issues (keeping students "on task" despite the lure of the Internet) (Kasowitz 2000, 19).

Although it may seem easy to look at online learning as a class by itself (pun intended!), actually online instructional experts say there really should be no difference at all. "A virtual classroom should not be much different from a real classroom—at least, not in the ways that count" (Porter 1997, 24). Whether online or "face to face," an effective classroom, Porter says, does the following:

- It provides the tools that learners need when they need them. If it's not possible to have all the tools in the classroom, an effective educator/trainer explains where the tools can easily be located.

- It creates an expectation for and an environment conducive to learning.

- It brings together educators/trainers and learners to share information and exchange ideas.

- It allows learners the freedom to experiment, test their knowledge, practice completing tasks, and apply what they've discussed or read about.

- It provides mechanisms for evaluating performance.

- It provides a safe haven in which learning can take place (Porter 2002, 24).

Understand and Overcome the Barriers

> I believe that human factors provide the most difficult barriers to successful online instruction. Many would like to focus on the technology. Remember, although technology glitches can occur, technology is only the tool that is being used! Students must be proactive to complete work and take advantage of the convenience of online instruction. On the other hand, teachers should make sure lessons are well organized and that instructions are clear. Confusion can result from a lack of effort in either area!

As you can see, there is virtually no difference between the expectations for an online course and those for a face-to-face course. It is simply up to the instructor to develop the course content that sets high expectations for learners and makes tools for learning easily and readily available.

Another teaching with technology issue that was a huge barrier for our school was the fact that students were not permitted to use e-mail at school! Because e-mail is the quickest and easiest way to communicate with online students, this was a huge problem for us! Luckily, ANGEL (our course development software) included a built-in e-mail system, so it all worked out. If your school does not allow e-mail, there are safe and monitored e-mail systems, like ePals (www.epals.com), that are affordable and safe.

To make sure you understand the barriers before "diving in" to online learning, ask yourself the following questions.

Survival Tips

- Do I have the technical support necessary to conduct an online course?

- Have I scheduled necessary blocks of time for course creation and planning?

- Have I thought of ways to avoid copyright violations and plagiarism issues?

- Have I considered Internet safety for students and provided ample security?

- Do I have a colleague to assist me in this endeavor?

- Does my school allow students to use e-mail for educational purposes? If not, have I thought of an alternative plan?

Survival Source 2

http://mnscsc.org/Socrates/elearning/downloads/probs_opps_ollchecklst.pdf

This site provides a survey listing the advantages of and challenges to online learning. It would be a handy survey to assess the teachers in your building to determine their readiness level regarding utilizing online courses with students.

Barriers	Solutions
Student Motivation and Progress—Successful online learning requires more independent learning and higher levels of self-motivation than a typical classroom. There is no teacher telling you what to do each day!	This number 1 barrier is best addressed with the right balance of reward and external motivation. Most students want the credit for completing the work. Set appropriate deadlines and targets with a balance of rewards and consequences in place.
Access (Internet and Computer)—This is an absolute. If you do not own a computer, you must access a computer in a library or a friend's house. You must also pay for Internet access unless you use a computer at school or the public library.	This, of course, is an absolute. The technology does not need to be new or fancy, just dependable. . . . Wayne Township recently started a program called BTG (Bridging the Gap) to place "replaced" district computers in homes of students who do not have computers.
Application Knowledge—Students must have basic knowledge of how to use a computer and use word processing software. Some assignments require moderate to advanced knowledge.	Basic knowledge is beneficial but not required. Students who are not comfortable with technology will have an uphill climb. This barrier is best addressed by providing links to online tutorials. I also suggest starting with small projects that build on early success. For example, start with a one-slide PowerPoint™ project before requiring multiple slides.
Setup (Logins, Access)—What is the Web site? How do students log in and access the material?	Clear and concise directions/orientation. Student logins should be easy to remember (i.e., match their school computer login). Create login cards with printed/posted directions on how to get started.
Instructional Design/Navigation—This is where the rubber meets the road! What standards should be covered? In what order?	Many students comment about whether a course was organized well. Their success seems to be tied to the ease with which they can navigate and understand the layout of the course content. Much time should be spent not only establishing an organized and easy to follow layout but also listening to student questions and complaints to continually improve the online material.
Fast-Paced Changes—Software, viruses, online access, and tools. The content created today will or should look different within a year!	Wow! Keeping up with the Joneses! This simply requires time and money to stay updated with all the new software and updated Web sites with new and improved technologies. Online courses and lessons should look different each year and really be overhauled every few years.

Survival Tool 2. Teaching Online: Problems and Solutions T-Chart

Barriers	Solutions
Formatting Web Pages—Web page creation in its basic form is completed by typing straight HTML code into a text document. Macromedia's Dreamweaver™ takes Web page design to new heights. Java and Flash also add to the interactivity of Web-based content.	Select a format with which you are comfortable and stay with it until a change become necessary. Beginners should stick with basic word processing applications that convert to HTML. Some Online Course Management Systems have HTML editors embedded within them (also a good choice). More advanced users can choose specific Web page editing applications like Dreamweaver or MS FrontPage™.
Updating Links—Links that do not work are called "broken" links. Avoid this at all costs since it makes your site look "broken!" Addresses to various Web sites change on a regular basis. Some Web sites are taken down after a certain amount of time.	Use one resource page, not scattered ones. Web page links change often. A list of twenty links may have five bad links after one year. Check and update these links on a regular basis. I keep an active Bookmark/Favorite List as I find links. I keep them organized by categories based on the courses I teach as well as for my roles at work.
Authenticity—If Johnny or Suzy is getting a grade, how do you know he or she is the one that completed the work? (Not that you don't trust those wonderful students that you teach each day!)	Another big one. Best addressed by requiring student presence at an exit assessment. No credit should be awarded unless the student shows proficiency.
How many more barriers should we list? The number one barrier for online students seems to be the possible lack of initiation and motivation to complete their work. An online course or set of lessons can be provided to any group of students in a school setting with the appropriate technology. But much like any typical classroom, five students will take off and complete the work with gusto, five will not get much done—no matter what you try—and the rest will plod along to get the work done because they have to. The most successful results occur when students are provided a time and place to work. Some students will have to be guided and prodded.	

Survival Tool 2. Teaching Online: Problems and Solutions T-Chart

Chapter 3

READ, RESEARCH, AND RESOURCES

Survival Strategy

The course is great! It helps me to remember library procedures and protocol. I enjoy doing this because it is preparing me for college. Research on the Internet has made students unfamiliar with the library setting. It helps to get back to the roots of research.—Joshua Coe, BDHS Senior **(Yippee! pb)**

This is the time when you will really begin to prepare yourself by researching and reading articles about Web-based training and online learning. This is a key time to begin gathering books on teaching with technology and surfing the Internet for related sites. Some of the best resources, which I found in my own by "surfing" and searching, are listed at the end of this chapter.

As you consider the available options, don't forget about the valuable resources in your own building—staff members who may have created, or who may be in the process of creating, their own online courses. Ask around—you might be able to learn from their mistakes and expertise!

Another great resource can be found by either physically visiting or virtually visiting a nearby college. Colleges have been using and taking advantage of distance learning opportunities for a number of years now. E-mailing a professor or department chair could prove advantageous as you're digging around for resources. In some cases, you can even virtually "visit" online classrooms by going in as a guest (this is discussed in greater detail in the next chapter). By observing how the course is set up, witnessing how the instructor gets students involved, and discovering what types of activities are included in the course, you'll have a better idea of how you want to structure your own course.

Survival Tips

1. **Blackboard's Support Site.** This site (http://www.blackboard.com) is an excellent starting point for your research. Helpful tip sheets and online support are available at the touch of a button. Online tutorials are also available to help you "get the feel" for online courses (http://www.blackboard.com/viewlets/). Blackboard's "10 Easy Steps to Put Your Course Online" is also an excellent diving-in spot (http://www.creighton.edu/Blackboard/10steps.html).

2. *Using the Big6 to Teach and Learn with the Internet.* This resource by Abby S. Kasowitz (Linworth, 2000) is invaluable. If time is short (and whose isn't!), focus on Chapter 4, "Designing and Providing Content on the Internet for K–12 Students."

3. *Creating the Virtual Classroom: Distance Learning with the Internet.* This helpful book, by Lynnette R. Porter (John Wiley & Sons, 1997), includes information on all aspects of online courses, such as supervising students, developing courses, and promoting your site.

4. **How to Develop an Online Course.** Although this site (http://stylusinc.com/online_course/tutorial/process.htm), which includes a step-by-step guide to developing an online course, can be a bit overwhelming because of its technical nature, I still found some good tidbits of information, especially in the Instructional Design section.

5. **Creating Online Courses: A Step-by-Step Guide.** Klemm's site (http://ts.mivu.org/default.asp?show=article&id=861) was one of the best I found in terms of user-friendliness and practical tips. If time is limited, just reading the conclusion's ten lessons is extremely worthwhile.

6. *The Online Educator: A Guide to Creating the Virtual Classroom.* Marguerita McVay Lynch's book (Falmer Press, 2002) provides straightforward, novice-friendly advice on how to develop an online course. Although quite costly ($124.95), this valuable resource is a must-have to get started.

Although many other Web sites, books, and articles are surfacing every day, these sources are enough to get you started in the right direction.

In the sources listed above you will most likely discover some differing viewpoints regarding online instruction. Just as teachers don't always agree about how best to teach in the "regular" classroom, there are many differing opinions when it comes to teaching online. In my own research, I discovered five common misconceptions that occurred over and over in the readings. Following are five popular myths about online education.

Myth 1: Online Learning Is Easy to Evaluate

Online schools have been in existence for many years now. Although it is difficult to compare online learning directly to a regular school setting, the comparison usually shows minimal difference in the outcomes. Of course, the convenience of online learning is well documented and can provide success to those who may have been unable to attend regular school.

Evaluation of online content and courses also presents some curious barriers. Mainly, how can you observe teaching and learning taking place? One solution for the Indiana Online Academy, an Indiana-based online high school program, is to gather student input. Students complete an online survey questionnaire anonymously. Ultimately, the comments viewed by teachers and administrators improve the content and instruction. This process is similar to what already occurs on college campuses on a regular basis.

Read, Research, and Resources

Where is the best information on online instruction? Online, of course! (You're probably thinking, "Duh!" right now, and wondering, if I'm such an online fan, why I'm even writing a book, but bear with me!) I wholeheartedly believe that books have their place and that all information cannot simply become "digital." That is why we will also have an online component to this book. Printed books can be updated and republished, but that takes time and may only happen after a few years. Like print, online resources can also become stagnant and dated, but the time needed to update them is significantly less—some of the more simpler updates can take place in minutes! Online tutorials may also have to be provided for those students who need instructions on the use of PowerPoint™, for example. Make sure to use the links that I've listed in appendix 3 to get very useful information on online instruction, online!

Myth 2: Online Education Saves Teachers Time

"Learning to work with online technology is time-consuming, difficult, and ultimately inconvenient. Some teachers clearly view preparing technologically supported lessons as a much greater demand on their time and energy than preparing a classroom activity without technology" (DiPetta et al. 2002, 25).

Certainly time will be saved in the future—once the course is up and running. The grading time alone, for example, will be considerably shortened if automated grading systems are used. But, as stated before, the start-up time is considerable.

Myth 3: Online Teaching Equals Better Learning

Information and communication technology can, and often does, provide a greater number of students with access to information that they may have been unable to access, but this is not to say that students are grasping and understanding the concepts involved. That's why it's critical to put quality evaluative tools in place throughout the unit. What—and how much—students learn is ultimately up to you. That's why an entire chapter here is devoted to course design and another to planning quality instruction.

Myth 4: Online Teaching Is Easier Than Traditional Teaching

Wrong! Just because you don't see your students face-to-face every day doesn't mean this instructional method is any easier than traditional teaching strategies. In fact, online teaching can be harder because building rapport and relationships online takes considerably more effort. Some online teachers have reported that, although online teaching is "ten times harder" than classroom teaching, they wouldn't have it any other way.

Myth 5: Online Teaching Is Best for Advanced Students

Wrong again! One of the best things about designing online courses is the ability to differentiate and plan lessons and activities for learners of all ability levels. In my online course, for example, the advanced students completed all ten "Giant Steps," while a basic English course completed seven of the ten steps. As in traditional instruction, sometimes modifications and adaptations are needed.

At a recent technology conference, survey results showed that online student success depends both on reading level and grade point average (GPA). In fact, students who read on grade level (or above) and have at least a 2.5 GPA (C average) tend to be successful. Students do not have to be on the honor roll or have technical supremacy to succeed in an online environment.

Survival Source 3

http://www.pitt.edu~poole/onlinelearning.htmldesigningOLactivities

The research and resources on this site are endless. Caution: Don't jump in if you are in a hurry!

Three to "Sea": Additional Resources to Keep You Afloat

Elbaum, Bonnie, Cynthia McIntyre, and Alese Smith. *Essential Elements: Prepare, Design, and Teach Your Online Course*. Madison, WI: Atwood Publishers, 2002.

Gilbert, Sara Dulaney. *How to Be a Successful Online Student*. New York: McGraw-Hill, 2000.

Hofmann, Jennifer. *The Synchronous Trainer's Survival Guide: Facilitating Successful Live and Online Courses, Meetings, and Events*. New York: Wiley, 2003.

Frequently Asked Questions—and Answers

As you begin to read about Pam's exploits regarding the use of "courseware" to create an online unit pertaining to library skills, you may have a few questions. In fact, you may have the same questions as many others. The answers to these frequently asked questions can be found below.

Q. How in the world do you get started?

A. It's simple! Just access online courseware like Blackboard or ANGEL (actually, you really could just post Web pages on the Internet). Of course you, should also know the content that you plan to teach!

Q. What is courseware?

A. ANGEL, Blackboard, and other tools are specifically designed for teachers of any content to control an online environment or "course." These online environments provide many tools for online learning (chat rooms, lesson pages, online calendar events, e-mail, and much more). The most amazing component is the ability to track or record student and teacher input and activity. In other words, a teacher knows when, what, and even how long a student has been working on the online course.

Q. How do you post content online?

A. You first need an Internet connection. In most cases, the courseware will have a location for you to click a button to create a page. The best tools allow you to simply copy and paste content from a Word document on your computer (onto the open space provided by the courseware). You may also choose simply to type your content into the forms provided.

Q. Do students need to log in?

A. It depends on how the pages are loaded. If your Web pages are uploaded to a secure site within courseware, the answer is yes. If the pages are simply loaded on the Internet for all to view, then the answer is no.

Q. Why should you use courseware?

A. Quite simply, courseware should be used for data and control. Courseware allows an online teacher to control *what* content can be accessed and even *when*. Most tools also allow passwords to be assigned for tests.

Q. Where do you find resources?

A. Pam and I prefer to use Google and Yahoo. It is important to enter selected words to find the right content. For K–12 content, make sure to list K12 in the search box! I find that many resources lead to other resources, so I start with an initial search and browse away, bookmarking as I go . . . .

Q. How does online instruction meet the needs of ALL students?

A. Online content is exceptionally useful for teaching alternative students. Courseware allows teachers to modify and store content in a variety of ways. There really is no limit!

Survival Tool 3. Just the FAQs!

Chapter 4

VIEW OTHER COURSES TO DETERMINE FORMAT

Survival Strategy

In other online courses I've taken, I found it hard to navigate. This course was very user-friendly!—Jeremy Barker, BDHS Senior (**Easy navigating is your roadmap to success! pb**)

In my case, deciding on a format was easy. Our school corporation had already purchased the ANGEL online course software. If online courses are new (or, in some cases, nonexistent), your school may not have a system in place. If that's the case, it's time to dive in and become familiar with what's out there.

To get acquainted with what's available, take a virtual field trip! Take a look around at other Web courses to get some general ideas at this preliminary stage. Some Web courses have restricted access (although most will allow you "in" if you request permission and advise them of your purpose); others have open access, allowing anyone entrance. As you're looking around, don't forget to peek around in your own building—or district—to see what might be going on right next door.

With the increasing popularity of online courses, software programs known as courseware are popping up. Courseware systems provide an Internet-based program to manage all aspects of online education, namely teaching and learning. Some tasks that courseware routinely performs are evaluating and grading, developing course rosters, and tracking course information. Courseware utilizes tools to facilitate learning by distributing course information, delivering instruction, and facilitating teacher–student interaction.

If your school corporation has already adopted courseware, it's best to use what's already in place. Students become familiar with a certain format, and the transition from course to course becomes easier. If you find, on the other hand, that the courseware simply will not work for you (or can't do what you want it to do), you have no other option than to go with one that will work for you—and your students.

As you're diving in to online courseware, here are some of the best starting points!

Survival Tips

1. Blackboard

    One of the most popular courseware tools, Blackboard, can be found at www.blackboard.com. The site hosts a variety of tools and offers a wealth of support for users. This site is probably the "Cadillac" of online course sites.

    Author's Note: Because of its wealth of resources, Blackboard's site can be tricky to navigate. Hang in there and be patient—the trip is worth it!

    Cost: Free 60-day trial

    $295 per year

2. Quia

    Another popular choice, Quia, is located at www.quia.com. Although it doesn't have all the bells and whistles that Blackboard has, this program is still a good bet and extremely affordable.

    Cost: $49 per year (per instructor)

3. ANGEL

    ANGEL (developed in 1996) is actually the second version of courseware developed for Indiana University-Purdue University Indianapolis (IUPUI). Our online school (IOA) uses this courseware. Many regular classroom teachers are now using it to support instruction and assessment in our classrooms.

    Cost: Free 30-day trial

    Price determined by needs

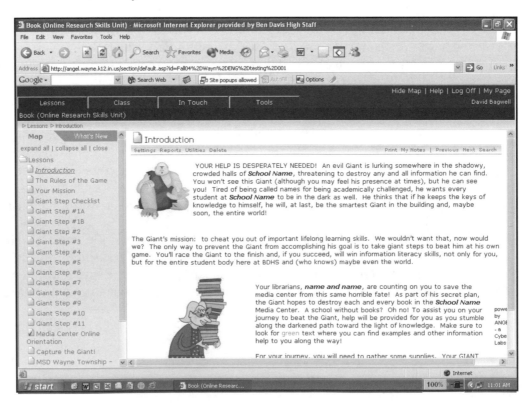

4.   Other

If you can't find or afford a courseware program to meet your specific needs, it's possible to create your own Web page using a program like FrontPage™ (www.Microsoft.com), Dreamweaver™ (www.macromedia.com), or Composer™ (www.netscape.com). If you're new to Web design, there are templates available to assist you. Templates simply allow you to fill in the blanks with your own content. "Quick and Dirty Web Pages" (http://www.elmhurst.edu/library/workshoppages/quickdirty00.html) is a lifesaver for beginners (like me!).

Microsoft Office™ also has tools that automatically convert Word documents, spreadsheets and even PowerPoint™ into Web pages. Just make sure you have a location to post your pages online (your technology department can help with this). Most schools have this ability, but there are also commercial entities that charge a fee to "host" your page. Another free option is to partner with a local college.

If you're like me, and Web designing is way over your head, consider asking around. Web design students or computer-savvy kids can be a great survival strategy!

Cost: FREE! (with software and tech-savvy student helpers).

Still can't make a decision on what courseware to use? You may want to go to the Edutools Web site (http://www.edutools.info) to explore other options. This site was created by WCET (Western Cooperative for Educational Telecommunications) specifically for those looking to acquire courseware. It is overloaded with reference materials, and the comparison chart is truly a survival tool!

No matter which format you ultimately choose, Survival Tool 4 is a handy checklist to use in your virtual visits.

View Other Courses to Determine Format (Virtual Visits)

IOA teachers meet annually to discuss and share experiences. One productive exercise has been to pair up and view the courses of a peer. Teachers learn a great deal from each other during this short discussion. We also connect new online teachers with experienced online teachers. Online instruction is unique and requires teachers to view their approach differently than they would when teaching in a walled classroom!

Survival Source 4

http://www.nwrel.org/mentoring/elearning.html

The National Mentoring Center is in the process of studying online learning formats and is dedicated to helping to improve the quality of online courses. Check out this site often for the latest research and findings.

When you check out a course site, note these items:

1. **Hardware**
   __ Special equipment is required to access the site.

   __ Learners can enter the site using different types of computers, with different operating systems.

   __ A dial-up connection is fast enough to work well with the site.

   __ A direct or dedicated line is required to work well with the site.

   __ A wireless connection is stable enough to work well with the site.

   __ The computer requires additional devices, such as sound or graphics cards, a CD player, or more memory, to access all materials.

   __ The computer does not require any special devices to access and play all materials.

   __ An older PC can be used by learners to complete this course.

   __ A brand-new PC can be used by learners to complete this course.

   Additional comments about hardware:

2. **Software**
   __ Specific browsers are recommended or required.

   __ Specific versions of one or more browsers are recommended or required.

   __ Any browser can be used to access course information.

   __ Required software is provided to learners online, on a floppy disk, or on a CD.

   __ Learners must provide their own software.

   __ Common versions of popular software are required for completing assignments or using materials.

   Additional comments about software:

Survival Tool 4. Notesheet for Evaluating Online Courses

3. **Networks and policies regarding their operation**

   __ Course or institutional networks seem secure.

   __ Course or institutional networks are easy to access and work well.

   __ Course sites include privacy and security statements.

   __ The institution's privacy and security policies are documented online.

Additional comments about networks and policies:

4. **Educational tools**

   __ Tools are easy to use, because they are intuitive or allow transfer of skills from learners using similar Web sites.

   __ New tools are explained and demonstrated at the site.

   __ Several tools are available for use with asynchronous learning or communication.

   __ Several tools are available for use with synchronous learning or communication.

   __ All tools work.

   Additional comments about educational tools:

5. **Types of materials and media**

   __ Different learning styles or preferences are incorporated into the course design.

   __ Multimedia are used frequently.

   __ Course materials are text or print based.

   __ Streaming information (audio and/or video) is available.

   __ Audio, video, graphic, and text files are available.

   __ Materials can be downloaded quickly.

   __If text files are printed, the average printout is a manageable size.

   __ The amount of linked material seems appropriate fro the length of the course and the subject matter.

Survival Tool 4. Notesheet for Evaluating Online Courses

___ The quality of the materials is high.

___ (It seems that) most materials have been created by the teacher or the course designer.

___ (It seems that) most materials have been taken from other sources.

___ Sources of information are documented or attributed properly.

___ The sources seem current and accurate and represent a variety of viewpoints.

___ The information seems timely.

___ The materials can be reused.

___ The materials can be used only in this course or only one time.

___ The online materials stand alone, without the need for a textbook, CD, or other supplementary materials.

___ Supplementary information is found in a textbook, CD, or other format.

Additional comments about types of materials and media:

6. **Number and types of assignments**

___ Assignments are listed in a course syllabus or schedule.

___ Point values, due dates, and descriptions are listed for each assignment.

___ The number of assignments seems reasonable for the length and depth of the course.

___ The number and type of assignments per week or learning module seems practical and reasonable.

___ The types of assignments reflect different learning styles or preferences.

___ Assignments are appropriate for studying the subject matter.

___ Assignments are appropriate for this educational level (e.g., an undergraduate university class, a postgraduate class, a noncredit professional development class).

___ Real-time and asynchronous assignments are required.

___ Instructions are provided so that learners know in what format the assignments should be completed.

___ Instructions are provided so that the learners know how to use plagiarism checking software or tools.

Survival Tool 4. Notesheet for Evaluating Online Courses

___ From the course site, learners know when they will receive feedback about the assignments and what type of responses they will receive (e.g., an e-mail message, a posted grade).

___ Policies about academic honesty, grade scales, and expectations for performance are listed on the course site.

Additional comments about number and types of assignments:

7. **Amount of required interaction with the material**

___ Learners are required to complete journals, workbooks, essays, research papers, or questionnaires.

___ Learners are required to participate in chat sessions, conference calls, or videoconferences.

___ Learners are required to send a certain number of e-mail messages or post so many comments on a bulletin board.

___ Learners are required to participate in lab sessions.

___ Learners demonstrate their mastery of the subject matter or a skill in several ways throughout the course. (These ways, not previously listed on the notesheet, include

_____

_____.)

Additional comments about required interaction with the material:

8. **Amount of required or encouraged interaction with others in the class**

___ Learners are required or encouraged to participate in group activities or projects.

___ Learners are required or encouraged to work alone on some or all assignments.

___ Outside assistance from mentors, colleagues, teachers, or other students is allowed or encouraged.

___ Learners are required to interview people outside the class.

Survival Tool 4. Notesheet for Evaluating Online Courses

___ Interpersonal contact is suggested or required between a learner and others inside and outside the class.

___ A specified amount of communication is required between the teacher and learners, and between the learner and others in the class.

___ The teacher's response time is reasonable and consistent.

___ Communication seems to be primarily asynchronous.

___ Communication seems to be primarily synchronous.

___ More than one communication method is used in the course. (Communication methods include _____

_____.)

Additional comments about required interaction with others:

9. **Evaluations**

___ Learners evaluate the course and teaching effectiveness at the end of the class.

___ Evaluations are confidential (according to privacy or security policies).

___ Evaluations are completed and submitted online.

___ Evaluations are completed and submitted other than online.

___ Evaluations require learners to select from multiple choice or other listed selections.

___ Evaluations allow learners to submit written comments.

___ Teachers see the evaluations. (You may not be able to learn this from the Web site, unless it is documented in a privacy or security statement.)

___ Others (e.g., administrators) see the evaluations. (You may not be able to learn this from the Web site, unless it is documented in a privacy or security statement.)

___ Evaluations are used to improve the course or curriculum. (You may not be able to learn this from the Web site, unless it is documented in a privacy or security statement.)

Additional comments about evaluations:

Survival Tool 4. Notesheet for Evaluating Online Courses

10. **Length of course and number of learners**

___ The length of the course seems appropriate for the amount and depth of information covered.

___ The class size seems appropriate for effective communication among learners and the teacher.

___ The class size seems manageable for the teacher, who has to read assignments, grade projects, etc.

___ The class size seems manageable for learners, who need to develop one or more learning communities as they study the subject matter.

___ The length of the course seems appropriate for the amount of credit given for the work.

___ The time frame seems appropriate for an online course.

Additional comments about length of course and number of learners:

Survival Tool 4. Notesheet for Evaluating Online Courses

Chapter 5

INSTRUCTION—PLAN ACTIVITIES, DEVELOP LESSONS, DECIDE ON COURSE CONTENT

Survival Strategy

I think that an online course is a good way to get acquainted with the media center, but there are still a few problems that I had. For example, when planning the unit, the directions should have been a little more detailed and clear.—Kristin Lucero, BDHS Sophomore **(Piloting the program will help you get the right balance between not being specific enough in your instructions and directions being too specific! pb)**

Planning for online instruction is no different than planning for traditional classroom instruction. You want students to be actively engaged in their learning. To meet this goal, you should plan high-quality, interactive lessons that require students to participate and make connections with what they're learning. Before I revised my unit, one of the most frequently used words in the evaluation was (unfortunately!) "boring." While I didn't think the lessons were boring, students wanted a lot less "talk" and a lot more "action!" One of the best sources I found to fill this missing link was *E-Learning Games* by Kathleen M. Iverson (Pearson, 2005).

Survival Tips

Iverson believes that, for online education to be successful, learning must be

- engaging and active (get students actively involved),
- positive and supportive (a caring, positive atmosphere),
- collaborative (cooperative and group learning), and
- contextual (relevant with real-life applications) (adapted from Iverson 2005, 1).

Further, when planning instruction, there are other things to consider:

1. Meaningful content (allows for a higher level of thinking).

2. Being thematic (making connections helps learners retain what they've learned).

3. Being exciting (use audio, music, movement, and graphics).

Taking the time to plan quality, interactive lessons is critical to a successful online course. For starters, plan an activity that helps students get to know each other—and you! One possibility is having students make an ID badge for themselves that they post online for others to view. The ID badge would contain the student's picture, e-mail address, and hobbies (adding the hobbies feature allows opportunities for student connections). Another opening activity is to get students used to online discussion boards by playing "Did I Lie?" To participate, students make up a crazy statement about themselves. Other students have to decide whether or not the statement is true.

Now that the students have gotten to know each other, it's time to plan your content-related lessons. You've decided on the *what*—now it's time for the *how*. How are you going to get students to learn (or master) the content? Whatever you do, don't make the same mistake I made and give too much discussion in the form of text. Text without graphics, movement, and activity is just like a teacher lecturing without stopping. And, what's worse, students don't even have the instructor to zone out on! It's a lot like the Charlie Brown teacher. You hear the words (or see the words in this case), but don't understand a thing. This can be true for online lessons—if you're not careful. For Giant Step 3, for example, I asked students to find three online database articles. To my dismay, students found this activity to be extremely boring. When I turned the activity into an online scavenger hunt to be completed with a partner, however, things suddenly changed! The students were learning the same content, but learning it in a team competition was much "funner."

Instruction—Plan Activities, Develop Lessons, Decide on Course Content

The importance of this topic related to online instruction cannot be over-emphasized. Effective online courses and lessons must take advantage of the interactivity provided by available technology. Lesson format can be as simple as the HTML links, the varied navigation possibilities of PowerPoint™, or advanced features on online courseware. Whatever type of online tool is used, lessons should not be limited to posting simple lessons or an online syllabus that instructs students to "Read the chapter and answer the questions!"

Become an expert in the online tool that you use. Immerse yourself in the program by using all of the available components. Don't be shy, ask questions! Call the Help Desk! Although it takes time now, investments made will pay off in future student success. Your course will become sought after and recommended. I use two very different courseware products and try to take advantage of what both offer. I find that although they are different, they also have many similarities. As I tell others when they seem impressed that I know so many things about certain technologies, "I too experienced a time when I knew little about this program." How did I learn about it? I dug in, started using it, and asked a lot of questions!

Including fun and excitement in your course or orientation is not to say that every lesson must be a fun-filled learning adventure. Rather, the point I'm trying to make is that a variety of instructional strategies should be used—both asynchronous and synchronous lessons, cooperative and individual activities, and short-term and long-term projects. You may also wish to choose a "hybrid" option that has proven to be very successful. The hybrid option includes a mix of online instruction and regular face-to-face meetings. The regular meetings are a helpful checkup at which the teacher can answer questions and clarify specific details and requirements.

Another reason it's important to include interactive assignments while you're planning your online unit is to avoid the isolation that can sometimes occur with Web-based instruction. By planning interactive assignments, you force students to communicate with each other on a regular basis. Survival Tool 5 is a lesson plan form to jot down ideas and activities.

No matter what learning activities you've planned, it's important to provide a course syllabus or outline for students to follow. When planning your course, it is important that your course "RISE" to the occasion:

R = RELEVANCE

> Show how instruction relates to the learner.
>
> Be an instructor who models lifelong learning.
>
> Build a strong relationship between course objectives and outcomes.
>
> Teach in a problem-based manner that applies knowledge to real-world applications.

I = INTEREST

> Vary content organization and presentation to avoid boredom.
>
> Use active voice and action words.
>
> Provide opportunities for students to interact with each other and you, the instructor.
>
> Use debate to get students actively involved.
>
> Utilize different learning styles.
>
> Encourage healthy competition between students.

S = SATISFACTION

> Provide opportunities for students to use new skills.
>
> Provide continual and timely feedback and reinforcement to learners.
>
> Provide ample positive feedback.
>
> Share exemplary work with students.

E = EXPECTANCY

> Make the course easy to navigate.
>
> Organize the text for easy readability.
>
> Follow good graphic and design principles (keep it simple, easy to navigate, user-friendly with color and lots of white space).
>
> Be explicit and up front regarding expectations of student participation and assignment quality (adapted from Lynch 2001, 21).

Survival Source 5

http://www.eduref.org/cgi-bin/lessons.cgi/Language_Arts

The Educator's Resource Guide includes a wealth of lesson plans and activities to view for course content ideas.

LESSON PLANNING DESIGN

Teacher: _____

Class/Period: _____

Unit: _____

Date(s): _____

MATERIALS:

_____

_____

_____

_____

_____

_____

_____

_____

Anticipatory Set—

Objectives and Purpose Standards-based—

Best-Shot Instruction—

Guided Practice—

Independent Practice—

Closure—

Assessment—

Correctives/Enrichment—

Survival Tool 5. Lesson Planning Sheet

Chapter 6

VISIT CLASSROOMS
AND PILOT PROGRAM
(PROMOTION)

Survival Strategy

I was glad to be in the first class to try the online orientation. We got to get out of class!—Jeremy Barker, BDHS Senior (**At least he's honest! pb**)

You've researched, you've planned, and you've planned, and you've planned—now it's finally time to get started (the fun part!). Chances are, you've got some pilot teachers in mind—an English buddy down the hall with whom you regularly team or maybe a newbie teacher whom you'd like to get to know. Either way, it's now time to get some teachers on board and test out this thing you've created. Here are my survival tips to get started.

Visit Classrooms and Pilot Program (Promotion)

I believe Pam was right to implement her program slowly and with caution. The eventual success of her program was the result of combined early and small successes. Teachers were able to become part of the "buy-in" process. An online course or unit is a complicated system of instructions, information, and human interaction. I am sure that teachers now guiding their students through the information skills unit would breathe a sigh of relief that they did not go through the early editions of the program along with numerous other classes. Pam prevented chaos by moving with a cautious and steady resolve, making improvements along the way until she felt comfortable that the unit was ready (not necessarily perfect) for large-scale implementation.

Survival Tips

- Send an e-mail to one, two, or three teachers asking them to participate in this pilot project.

- Don't bite off more than you can chew—if you can only work with one teacher right now, that's fine. It would be better to have one quality pilot project than three chaotic ones. Remember, you're still trying to promote the program. You want it to be an organized, successful unit so that you can get more teachers on board for the next go-round!

- For the pilot project, offer to do all the grading. (No, I'm not crazy!) Obviously, you won't be able to offer this service during full-blown implementation, but for now just use the bait and switch strategy.

- During the pilot project, schedule the pilot class or classes weekly. You won't have to do more than touch base with the students (remember, it's an independent project), but until the teachers better understand the process, touching base weekly and doing a little cheerleading is very helpful.

- Have the teacher decide NOW how much the unit will count. Will it count as a test grade—or a quiz grade? I do not recommend just offering the project as extra credit because you won't get a lot of student participation that way.

- Many students want to know WHY you're doing this—be ready to be positive, yet direct, and most will come around.

Survivor Tool 6a is an introductory PowerPoint™ lesson for you for the pilot kickoff. Before showing the PowerPoint lesson, follow these steps:

- Give each student a folder. Put login instructions, handouts, and important notes in the folder. Students keep these folders throughout the unit to organize information they're collecting along the journey.

- Make sure students put their names on the folders right away! While it sounds simplistic, I've spent a lot of time trying to get folders back into the right hands—especially when a lot of completed work is inside. It's not as hard when you're only working with one class, but when you've got three or four going, it's tough!

- Be ready to monitor and adjust. For example, one lower-level class simply could not handle getting three database articles (actually, getting one was like pulling teeth!). For this class, I was forced to make some immediate modifications. Another class, an advanced course, simply found many of the lessons too easy. As a result, I had to make some in-flight adjustments to make the unit more interesting and challenging. (Jacob was one of these students—refer back to the Survival Strategy in chapter 5.)

- Solicit feedback throughout the course. Listen to what the kids (and teachers) are saying.

- Have a deadline from the first day. In fact, have multiple deadlines and target dates along the way so students can measure their progress as they work. If students don't have a deadline, they'll procrastinate (just like us!). Give realistic deadlines and try to stick with them as much as possible.

- Give yourself ample time to grade folders. If you wait until too close to the end of the grading period, you'll make it harder on the classroom teacher who needs the grade report. I would suggest regular grading (even daily) so that it does not become burdensome. Also, you'll want to give extra time for students to redo folders that don't meet your expectations.

- Remember, a completed folder is the student's "ticket for the test." No folder, no ticket (Survival Tool 6b is "just the ticket!") .

- Because I believe in mastery learning, I allow students to take the test until they pass it. You'll have to decide whether or not you will allow students to retest.

Survival Source 6

http://www.keele.ac.uk/depts/aa/landt/links/POTguidelines.htm

This site includes some important points for peer observations—important guidelines when visiting other teachers' classrooms and/or reviewing a peer's program.

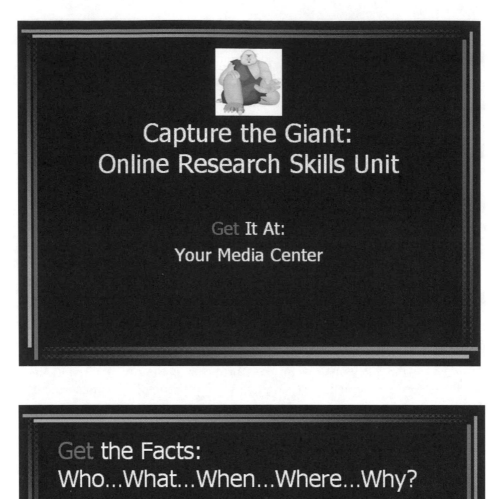

Survival Tool 6a. Giant PowerPoint Presentation

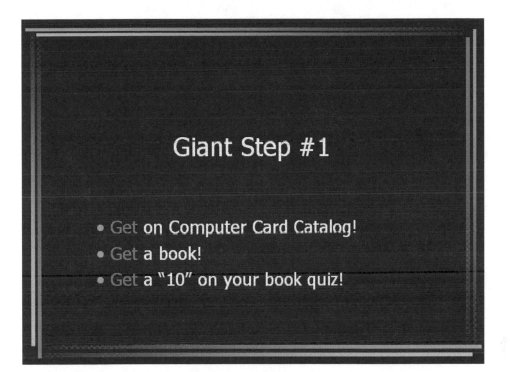

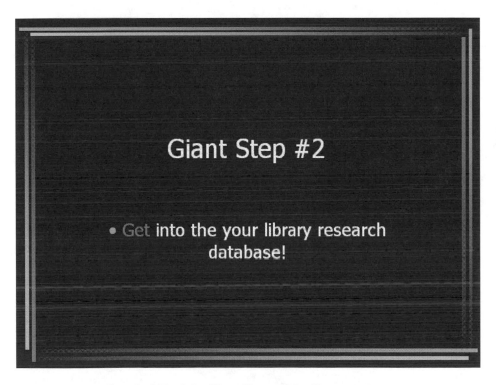

Survival Tool 6a. Giant PowerPoint Presentation

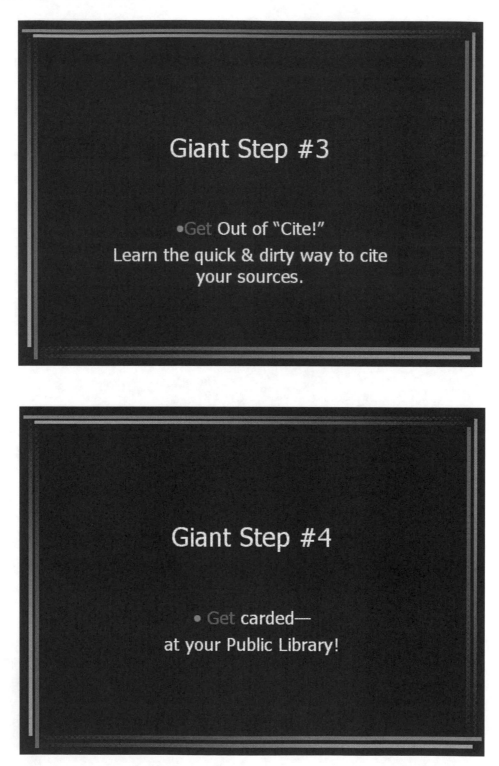

Survival Tool 6a. Giant PowerPoint Presentation

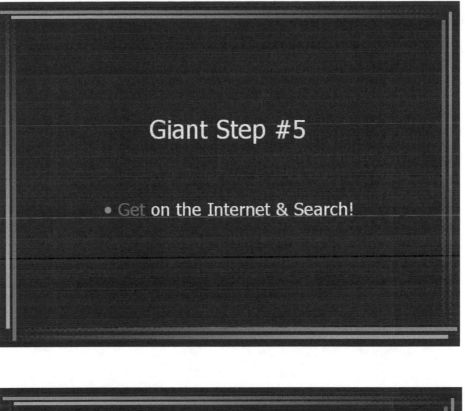

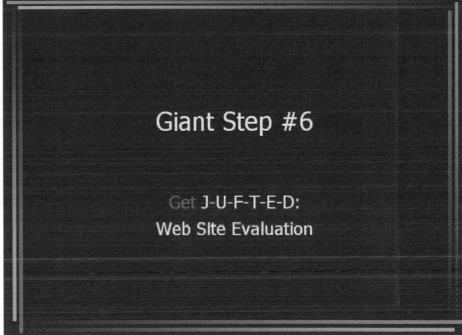

Survival Tool 6a. Giant PowerPoint Presentation

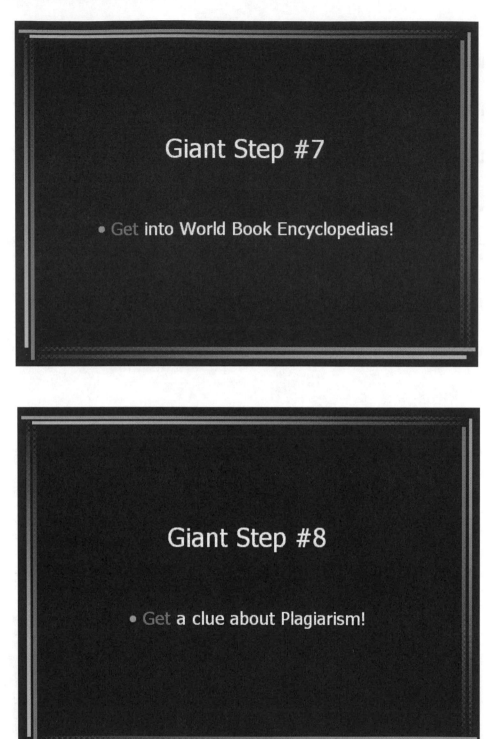

Survival Tool 6a. Giant PowerPoint Presentation

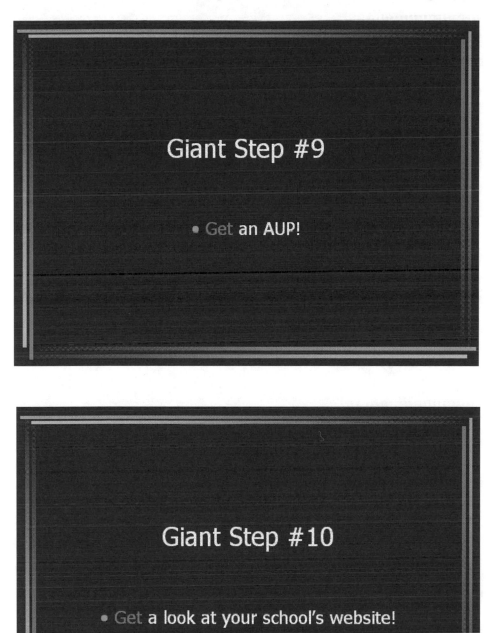

Survival Tool 6a. Giant PowerPoint Presentation

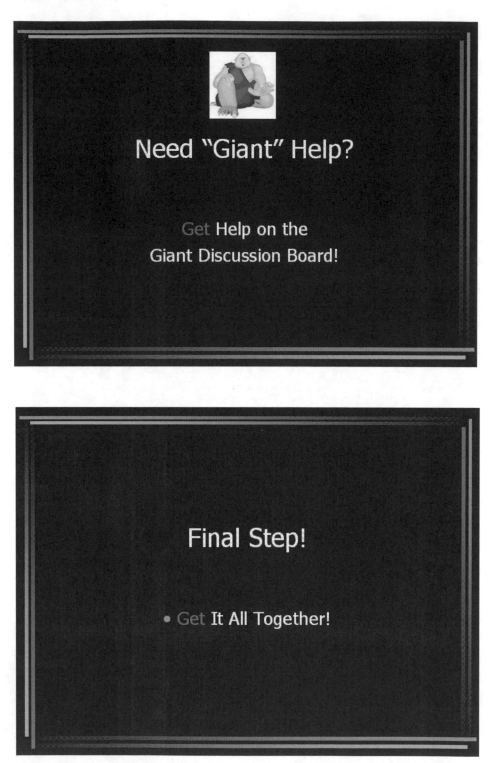

Survival Tool 6a. Giant PowerPoint Presentation

Media Center Online Orientation
TEST TICKET

Your GIANT Key to the Information Age!

Name: _____

Password: _____

Media Center Online Orientation
TEST TICKET

Your GIANT Key to the Information Age!

Name: _____

Password: _____

Media Center Online Orientation
TEST TICKET

Your GIANT Key to the Information Age!

Name: _____

Password: _____

Media Center Online Orientation
TEST TICKET

Your GIANT Key to the Information Age!

Name: _____

Password: _____

Survival Tool 6b. Ticket for the Test

Chapter 7

ADAPT UNIT TO MEET INDIVIDUAL NEEDS— DIFFERENTIATE!

Survival Strategy

I think I would do better if I worked with a partner!—Allison Tyler, BDHS Sophomore **(Remember to differentiate and account for different learning styles! pb)**

When I first designed the "Capture the Giant" unit, I pretty much thought of it as a "one size fits all" program. I had designed ten quality lessons and thought that the planning was basically done. Boy, was I wrong! Just like with my other instructional units, I found it necessary not only to adapt the curriculum to meet individual needs but to specifically differentiate and modify pieces of the unit to meet the varied individual needs of the students. For example, I found that some students needed to work through the units in partners in order to have the interpersonal time to communicate and share ideas, while others needed a more intrapersonal approach and preferred to work independently throughout the unit, requiring very little interaction with their fellow students, the instructor, or me. I discovered that often the different make-ups and climates of the class helped me to determine the best teaching strategy and differentiation methods to use. In some cases, remedial classes required me to demonstrate, model, and even provide a sample finished product on the presentation screen while they worked on the task. However, enrichment students really didn't even need me in the room! They were able to tackle the project with little or no direction, preferring to work at their own pace, and they provided me with excellent feedback on how the unit could be revised to be even better. Sound impossible? Not really. This chapter's survival tool will show you how you can easily ADAPT to meet the needs of your learners.

Adapt Unit to Meet Individual Needs—Differentiate!

Computer-based and online instruction is a fertile environment for differentiated instruction. Not only can various options be explored, but online assessment tools can be customized to react to student needs and even direct instruction to appropriate avenues. IOA teachers use the feedback component of the online quiz tool in ANGEL to steer students to appropriate resources, depending on student responses. Another strength of online courseware is the ability to provide personalized and automated instruction—a powerful combination!

Although you may not see students face-to-face, it is very important to develop a positive relationship with them. Just as in the regular classroom, there are always students who are intrinsically motivated and turn in quality work regularly—and on time. And, just as in the regular classroom, there are those reluctant learners who won't turn in work regularly and—when they do turn it in (usually late)—the work is of poor quality. Getting to know your students on a one-to-one basis can help those students who may otherwise "fall through the cracks." Here are some helpful tips:

- Get to know the students. Arrange a face-to-face meeting for the class kickoff.

- Ask for a short autobiographical paragraph for the first assignment.

- Communicate, communicate, communicate! Call home and e-mail to introduce yourself and establish personal contact.

- If a student has not been participating, call immediately! He or she may be struggling with the class—or it could be a simple computer glitch. Find out before the student gets too behind—and frustrated.

- Ask students to post their photographs and a few hobbies online.

- Be actively involved and a cheerleader for your students—and your course!

- Establish regular "office hours" for students who have questions or would rather meet with you face-to-face instead of via e-mail conferences.

- Share relevant personal information with your students—let them get to know you!

- If you know a student is at-risk, make sure he or she has the tools to be successful. At-risk students can have additional learning hurdles to overcome (no home computer, low motivation, low frustration threshold, poor written and verbal communication skills, poor study habits . . .). Any preparation you can do beforehand to help an at-risk student be successful is critical.

Survival Tips: Ten Differentiation Strategies

1. Know your students! Survival Tools 7a, 7b, and 7c are differentiation tools to help you identify needs of individual groups.

2. Find available resources to modify instruction.

3. Build a "toolkit" containing a variety of lessons at different levels so that differentiation requires very little time.

4. Use available technology to assist with differentiation needs.

5. Model instruction, (At BDHS we use the classroom PresenStation. For more information, go to http://www.wayne.k12.in.us/ois/presenstation.htm.)

6. If students finish early, provide enrichment opportunities in the form of links. For example, CyberDewey is an excellent resource to help students understand and "survive" the Dewey Decimal System (http://www.anthus.com/CyberDewey/CyberDewey.html). For a list of other resources to help you differentiate your online instruction, see appendix 11.

7. Provide a discussion board at which students can provide information regarding their individual needs and get help from their peers.

8. Collaborate with colleagues on suggestions for students who might be struggling with the unit, finding out their strengths and weaknesses in other subject areas.

9. Find a new "expert." Have students share in the presentation of unit examples and ask students to prepare additional "Giant Steps" they would like to see incorporated into the unit.

To make it easy to ADAPT, remember . . .

A Adapt curriculum to needs of students.

D Differentiate and modify.

A Access available resources and technology.

P Plan ahead so you won't be behind!

T Talk to the teacher to get critical class information.

Survival Source 7

http://www.support4learning.org.uk/education/lstyles.htm

This site provides countless resources and information on differentiation strategies, learning styles, and multiple intelligences.

TEACHER: _____

PERIOD: _____ SEMESTER: _____ YEAR: _____

DIFFERENTIATION STRATEGIES FOR GIANT STEP NUMBER _____

TOTAL NUMBER OF STUDENTS: _____

NUMBER OF ADVANCED STUDENTS: _____

NUMBER OF SPECIAL NEEDS STUDENTS: _____

NUMBER OF ENL STUDENTS: _____

****

NOTES:

Survival Tool 7a. Differentiation Checklist

SURVIVAL STRATEGY QUESTIONS

1. In what ways could the unit be shortened? Is it possible for special needs students to skip certain steps? If so, which ones?

2. Is it possible for accelerated students to pretest and test out of the unit?

3. What enrichment activities could students do who test out of the unit?

4. How might students be grouped for certain "Giant Steps?"

5. What will the teacher's role be in facilitating the unit and helping with differentiation activities?

****

NOTES:

Survival Tool 7b. Differentiation Questions

"Capture the Giant" Online Orientation Differentiation Strategies for Each Giant Step

Giant Step 1:

- Higher ability students can locate their own books—and then assist lower ability students with finding books.

- For lower ability students, highlight the specific section on the map where the students can locate their books.

Giant Step 2:

- Lower ability students could be allowed to find only one article, which can be saved as a favorite for easier searching.

- Higher ability students could find an additional article—or again assist other students in locating database articles.

Giant Step 3:

- Lower ability students will need to have the citation page bookmarked for them. Choose an easy book for students to cite that includes all the necessary information, to avoid confusion.

- For higher ability students, print off a citation and ask students to label the different parts of the printed citation.

Giant Step 4:

- Lower ability students may need additional assistance upon visiting the public library for the first time. Call ahead and make arrangements with a library staff member.

- Higher ability students can search the public library site ahead of time, reserve materials, and even complete a library card application in advance.

Giant Step 5:

- Lower ability students can compare two search engines (with assistance).

- Higher ability students can compare four or more search engines.

Giant Step 6:

- Assign Web sites for lower ability students. Students should be able to locate three factual key facts rather than evaluate sources.

- Higher ability students should find an example of each of the "JUFTED" criteria.

Survival Tool 7c. Differentiating Instruction Strategies

Giant Step 7:

- Lower ability students might use the Word "Auto Summarize" feature to locate key encyclopedia article information.

- Higher ability students can compare two print and online encyclopedia sources and create a Venn Diagram.

Giant Step 8:

- Lower ability students could be allowed to write five bulleted facts about plagiarism.

- Higher ability students could create a PowerPoint™ presentation on the dangers of plagiarism.

Giant Step 9:

- Lower ability students can read a highlighted AUP for the basics.

- Higher ability students could form cooperative groups and write their own mini-AUP to share with the class.

Giant Step 10:

- Lower ability students can answer questions about the Web site.

- Higher ability students could suggest additions and/or revisions to the media center Web site.

Survival Tool 7c. Differentiating Instruction Strategies

Chapter 8

LISTEN TO FEEDBACK

Survival Strategy

The directions for the online steps were a little unclear.—Allison Tyler, BDHS Sophomore (**Remember, what's crystal clear to you might not be to students! Are we clear on this? pb**)

No Comment!—Blake Vanderbush, BDHS Sophomore (**Hmmm . . . pb**)

Even though we don't always want to hear constructive criticism, in most cases this type of input can be invaluable in making improvements. And, if we're not hearing anything back, that's feedback in itself. The message is clear—you have to find out what students are saying—or thinking in this case!

Feedback lets you gain valuable insight into making a great lesson even better. There are many ways to gain feedback. Feedback can range from informal conversations in the hallway with a teacher to formal written evaluation. Feedback strategies, such as the "three plusses and a wish" chart (where the responder lists three good "things" and one thing he or she would like to change) or even a sticky note with feedback listed, are excellent ways to solicit input on your program. Students are often surprised when a teacher asks them for feedback and opinions on a lesson. They are even more surprised when that feedback is actually incorporated into subsequent lessons. Student reflections can be invaluable when deciding on the strengths and weaknesses of a unit and refining lesson strategies. An administrator (like Dave!) can also be an important person to give feedback and make suggestions for lesson improvements while not being in an evaluative role. No matter who gives you feedback, it's important to LISTEN. (Survival Tool 8 is a tool to gather feedback.)

Listen to Feedback ————————————————————

> Listening really is a skill that should be developed. Too often, we are concerned simply with our next move or comment. The second part of this chapter also needs a healthy dose of consideration and feedback. The importance of feedback is related directly to the success of the program. Perhaps most important, listening to feedback should lead to a response or action. Negative feedback can give rise to positive changes—and positive feedback can lead to celebration!

Survival Tips

L   Listen to feedback from teachers and administrators.

I   Initiate conversation with students to get feedback (See Survival Tool 8).

S   Stop and analyze responses without getting defensive.

T   Talk to others (who might be more objective) to see if feedback is valid.

E   Evaluate feedback and use it to plan new ideas and instructional strategies.

N   Note positive feedback and celebrate your successes.

Survival Source 8

http://www.yale.edu/ynhti/pubs/A14/polio.html

This site concurs that student feedback is all too often left out of evaluation. It also clarifies the roles of various stakeholders in the online learning game.

Capture the Giant: Online Research Skills Unit
Pilot Project—Feedback Form

Name _____ Period _____

Teacher _____ Date _____

Please check all that apply!

_____ I do have a project folder.

_____ I do NOT have a project folder.

_____ I DID have a project folder—I need another one!

_____ I have taken the reading test to determine my reading level. Score: _____

_____ I have taken a book quiz over a novel. Score: _____

_____ I am currently on Giant Step _____.

Comments and Feedback:

(Please list 3 "Giant" suggestions for improving the unit and 1 positive note below!)

Giant Suggestion 1:

Giant Suggestion 2:

Giant Suggestion 3:

Positive Note:

Survival Tool 8. Feedback Form

Chapter 9

GRADING—GET A PLAN!

Survival Strategy

I don't know what my score is!—Ben Stevens, BDHS Senior (**Give grades regularly! pb**)

I've certainly learned some important lessons when it comes to grading! No doubt about it, grading takes time. In the best-case scenario, all grading is automated. In the worst-case scenario, all lessons must be hand graded. Even automated grading systems require time to organize, record, and distribute results to students. With a little preplanning, though, even manual grading systems can be made a little less labor-intensive.

Survival Tips

- Set deadlines and stick to them whenever possible.

- Be flexible with students who have legitimate, valid reasons (like computer glitches) for turning in late assignments.

- Don't procrastinate! Keep up with the grading before it piles up and gets out of control.

- Whenever possible, have the computer auto grade assignments. The biggest problem is that, to be computer graded (and thus provide immediate feedback to students), many assignments must be objective. It's sometimes hard to make a quality evaluation fit the generic true-false or multiple choice format. If you can get your evaluation to fit this format, however, valuable time will be saved.

- Stagger due dates for classes to ensure you have time to finish grading assignments for one class before getting bogged down with another.

- If automated grading is not an option, use the old standby—Scantrons!

- Use checkmarks or pass/fail grading for "little assignments. (These nongraded assignments can be prerequisites for other graded assignments.)

- Use rubrics (like Survival Tools 9a and 9b) to simplify the grading process. (Provide rubrics to students prior to the due date so they know exactly what's expected.) For a rubric survival tool to help you easily develop rubrics online, go to http://www.rubistar.com.

- When possible, use student assistants to grade objective lessons.

- Give continual grading feedback to students to avoid "surprises" later.

- Rather than get overwhelmed with checking e-mail and grading posted assignments on a continual basis, set specific times that you will grade work—and evaluate only during those times. Otherwise, the technology can overwhelm you and you'll find valuable time being eaten up. Scheduling a block of time and maintaining the schedule will help make this step a little more manageable. I've always graded student work at the end of the day. You may choose to grade in the morning. Whatever time you choose, a daily plan is best so that you do not have a mountain of work to grade!

Grading: Get a Plan!

> When I am teaching my online class, I try to log in daily to pace myself and not get behind. The importance of timely grading lies in the fact that grading is actually teacher feedback to the students! Frequent teacher interaction through grading often can lead to improved student progress. Many students turn in work and "wait" for a response. From my experience, I have learned that students not only want, but need, confirmation that they are working correctly. I tie checking e-mail and grading assignments together as far as having a plan. In fact, I often incorporate e-mail as part of the course and "grade" e-mails that students send.

Want your students to make the "grade?" Kelly Rich, online instructor, has some "A+" strategies to help!

G   Grading Scale

Will the online course follow the same grading scale as the "regular" school, or is there a separate grading system for this course? Will grades be based on ability? How will special education students be graded? These are all things to consider before you get out the red pen!

R   Revising Assignments

Do teachers have the discretion to decide whether or not they want to have teachers revise assignments for an improved grade? If students can revise assignments, grading must be protected within the online environment. This is especially important when automated grading systems are used. For example, you don't want students receiving all of the correct answers prior to revising!

A   Assessments

When designing assessments, use rubrics and give students very clear guidelines about what will be expected of them. Following this procedure will make grading easier and much less controversial.

D   Deadlines

Deadlines keep students on task. Online or not, students often delay working on assignments when no clear deadline is given. Because you don't see online students every day, procrastination is an even bigger challenge.

E   Evaluation by Peers

Before students turn in graded assignments, allow them to "swap" assignments with a peer via e-mail. Students value opinions of other students.

Survival Source 9

http://www.findarticles.com/p/articles/mi_mOJSD/is_9_58/ai_79006750/pg 2

Will your online course make the "grade" when your administrator dives into your online course? Check out this site to find out!

Online Unit Grading Sheet
"Capture the Giant!"

Name: _____

Teacher: _____ Period: _____

****

Folder Turned In (On Time!) _____

Points on Folder _____

Computer Quiz (Bonus) _____

Online Final _____ (100)

Online Unit Final Grade _____

Total Points Possible _____

Survival Tool 9a. Grading Sheet

GIANT STEP 1	Record information on book checked out: Title, Author, Call Number, Barcode, Due Date	Document
	How many different titles by your favorite author does the Media Center have?	Document
GIANT STEP 1B	Book quiz	Folder
GIANT STEP 2	Three articles printed out from library research databases	Folder
	Citation information for all three articles	Document
GIANT STEP 3	Citation Maker printout	Folder
	Works cited page	Document
GIANT STEP 4	Copy of public library card	Folder
GIANT STEP 5	Go Ask Alice article	Folder
	Chart of Internet search results	Document
GIANT STEP 6	Copy of Internet page used for "JUFTED" activity	Folder
	"JUFTED" answers	Document
GIANT STEP 7	World Book Online article about "Giants"	Folder
	Page where "Giant" article appears in print version of *World Book Encyclopedia.*	Document
GIANT STEP 8	Plagiarism paragraph	Document
GIANT STEP 9	AUP—printed and signed	Folder
GIANT STEP 10	Media Center hours	Document
	20 T/F questions about Media Center procedures	Document

Cross out the word Document *or* Folder *when the task has been completed.*

Survival Tool 9b. Grading Checklist

Chapter 10

UNWRAP THE STANDARDS

Survival Strategy

The project, from my perspective, is beneficial and useful to those who need to learn the proper way to research. The steps are simple to follow, yet still effective. It also creates an atmosphere of intriguing learning while still ensuring we're meeting standards.—J. E., BDHS Senior (**Wow! A student who "gets it!" pb**)

Like it or not, standards are here to stay. Schools are being held more accountable than ever before to align with standards, provide data, and demonstrate mastery. If your program isn't standards-based and data-driven, then it's time to get with the program! The "Capture the Giant" unit is tied to the Information Literacy Standards, Big6 Skills, and language arts standards. Survival Tool 10 is a checklist to help make sure all standards are met—and help you track *which* lessons include *which* standards, helping you be intentional, aligned, and focused. Like mine, your program needs to have HIGH standards!

Survival Tips

H   Have copies of all standards accessible as you plan your lessons.

I   Incorporate the Big6 skills throughout your unit.

G   Gather information from teachers to make sure the most important language arts standards are integrated into your orientation unit.

H   Hold students accountable in meeting the standards—make sure they master each step and spiral the standards to make sure all are equally covered.

As do traditional classrooms, online courses also teach to the standards and many, if not all, follow a curriculum. For example, when I developed an online English course for our high school, specifically a novel unit, I had to adhere to the same standards and curriculum as those teachers who developed "regular" courses. In developing an online research unit, it is critical that you have the standards at hand and ready. Your entire course should be developed around the nine Information Literacy Standards, the Big6 skills, and your school's language arts standards. As you will see in part II of this book, each of my lessons matches one or more of these—they were my "road map" to the final destination.

Unwrap the Standards ────────────────

As Pam states, it's important to build any online course or lesson around the standards for the topic to be learned. The standards should actually become the foundation upon which one "builds" the units of instruction. The first instruction given to IOA teachers when they are creating an online course is to start with the state standards. Finally, it is important to note that this chapter and chapter 1 should be closely connected. The standards should definitely be included as part of the objectives and goals for the online instruction being developed. Doing so guarantees that standards become the foundation of the course, and success should soon follow!

Survival Source 10

http://www.awesomelibrary.org/Office/Teacher/Standards/Standards.html

The Awesome Library site includes valuable information from the U.S. Department of Education outlining the process for developing and implementing standards-based units.

Giant Step # **1**	Information Literacy Standards	The Big6 Skills	Language Arts (High School)
Searching and Book Checkout	**Information Literacy (Standard 1)**	**1. Task Definition**	Standard 1: Vocabulary Development
	Information Literacy (Standard 2)	2. Information Seeking Strategies	**Standard 2: Reading—Comprehension**
	Information Literacy (Standard 3)	3. Location and Access	Standard 3: Reading—Literary Response
	Independent Learning (Standard 4)	4. Use of Information	**Standard 4: Writing—Process**
	Independent Learning (Standard 5)	5. Synthesis	**Standard 5: Writing—Applications**
	Independent Learning (Standard 6)	6. Evaluation	Standard 6: English Language Conventions (Grammar)
	Social Responsibility (Standard 7)		Standard 7: Listening & Speaking
	Social Responsibility (Standard 8)		
	Social Responsibility (Standard 9)		

Survival Tool 10. Standards Chart

Excerpted from Chapter 2, "The Information Literacy Standards for Student Learning," of *Information Power: Building Partnerships for Learning*, by American Association of School Librarians and Association for Educational Communications and Technology. Copyright ©1998 American Library Association and Association for Educational Communications and Technology. Reprinted by permission of the American Library Association. The Big6 Skills are used and adapted with permission. The Big6™ is copyright ©1987 Michael Eisenberg and Robert E. Berkowitz.

Note: Standards in boldface type apply specifically to the Giant Step on that page of the chart.

Giant Step # **2**	Information Literacy Standards	The Big6 Skills	Language Arts (High School)
Advanced Searching Online Databases	**Information Literacy (Standard 1)** **Information Literacy (Standard 2)** **Information Literacy (Standard 3)** **Independent Learning (Standard 4)** Independent Learning (Standard 5) Independent Learning (Standard 6) Social Responsibility (Standard 7) Social Responsibility (Standard 8) Social Responsibility (Standard 9)	**1. Task Definition** **2. Information Seeking Strategies** **3. Location and Access** 4. Use of Information **5. Synthesis** 6. Evaluation	Standard 1: Vocabulary Development **Standard 2: Reading—Comprehension** Standard 3: Reading—Literary Response Standard 4: Writing—Process Standard 5: Writing—Applications Standard 6: English Language Conventions (Grammar) Standard 7: Listening & Speaking

Survival Tool 10. Standards Chart

Excerpted from Chapter 2, "The Information Literacy Standards for Student Learning," of *Information Power: Building Partnerships for Learning*, by American Association of School Librarians and Association for Educational Communications and Technology. Copyright ©1998 American Library Association and Association for Educational Communications and Technology. Reprinted by permission of the American Library Association. The Big6 Skills are used and adapted with permission. The Big6™ is copyright ©1987 Michael Eisenberg and Robert E. Berkowitz.

Note: Standards in boldface type apply specifically to the Giant Step on that page of the chart.

Giant Step # 3	Information Literacy Standards	The Big6 Skills	Language Arts (High School)
Get INSPIRED—Using Indiana's Virtual Library Database	**Information Literacy (Standard 1)**	**1. Task Definition**	Standard 1: Vocabulary Development
	Information Literacy (Standard 2)		Standard 2: Reading—Comprehension
	Information Literacy (Standard 3)	**2. Information Seeking Strategies**	Standard 3: Reading—Literary Response
	Independent Learning (Standard 4)	**3. Location and Access**	Standard 4: Writing—Process
	Independent Learning (Standard 5)	**4. Use of Information**	Standard 5: Writing—Applications
	Independent Learning (Standard 6)		Standard 6: English Language Conventions (Grammar)
	Social Responsibility (Standard 7)	**5. Synthesis**	Standard 7: Listening & Speaking
	Social Responsibility (Standard 8)	6. Evaluation	
	Social Responsibility (Standard 9)		

Survival Tool 10. Standards Chart

Excerpted from Chapter 2, "The Information Literacy Standards for Student Learning," of *Information Power: Building Partnerships for Learning*, by American Association of School Librarians and Association for Educational Communications and Technology. Copyright ©1998 American Library Association and Association for Educational Communications and Technology. Reprinted by permission of the American Library Association. The Big6 Skills are used and adapted with permission. The Big6™ is copyright ©1987 Michael Eisenberg and Robert E. Berkowitz.

Note: Standards in boldface type apply specifically to the Giant Step on that page of the chart.

Giant Step # 4	Information Literacy Standards	The Big6 Skills	Language Arts (High School)
Get Carded—At Your Local Public Library	**Information Literacy (Standard 1)**	**1. Task Definition**	Standard 1: Vocabulary Development
	Information Literacy (Standard 2)		**Standard 2: Reading— Comprehension**
	Information Literacy (Standard 3)	**2. Information Seeking Strategies**	Standard 3: Reading—Literary Response
	Independent Learning (Standard 4)	**3. Location and Access**	Standard 4: Writing—Process
	Independent Learning (Standard 5)		
	Independent Learning (Standard 6)	**4. Use of Information**	**Standard 5: Writing— Applications**
	Social Responsibility (Standard 7)	**5. Synthesis**	Standard 6: English Language Conventions (Grammar)
	Social Responsibility (Standard 8)		
	Social Responsibility (Standard 9)	6. Evaluation	**Standard 7: Listening & Speaking**

Survival Tool 10. Standards Chart

Excerpted from Chapter 2, "The Information Literacy Standards for Student Learning," of *Information Power: Building Partnerships for Learning*, by American Association of School Librarians and Association for Educational Communications and Technology. Copyright ©1998 American Library Association and Association for Educational Communications and Technology. Reprinted by permission of the American Library Association. The Big6 Skills are used and adapted with permission. The Big6™ is copyright ©1987 Michael Eisenberg and Robert E. Berkowitz.

Note: Standards in boldface type apply specifically to the Giant Step on that page of the chart.

Giant Step #	Information Literacy Standards	The Big6 Skills	Language Arts (High School)
5 Online Searching	**Information Literacy (Standard 1)**	**1. Task Definition**	**Standard 1: Vocabulary Development**
	Information Literacy (Standard 2)	**2. Information Seeking Strategies**	**Standard 2: Reading Comprehension**
	Information Literacy (Standard 3)	**3. Location and Access**	Standard 3: Reading—Literary Response
	Independent Learning (Standard 4)	**4. Use of Information**	**Standard 4: Writing—Process**
	Independent Learning (Standard 5)	**5. Synthesis**	**Standard 5: Writing—Applications**
	Independent Learning (Standard 6)	**6. Evaluation**	**Standard 6: English Language Conventions (Grammar)**
	Social Responsibility (Standard 7)		Standard 7: Listening & Speaking
	Social Responsibility (Standard 8)		
	Social Responsibility (Standard 9)		

Survival Tool 10. Standards Chart

Excerpted from Chapter 2, "The Information Literacy Standards for Student Learning," of *Information Power: Building Partnerships for Learning*, by American Association of School Librarians and Association for Educational Communications and Technology. Copyright ©1998 American Library Association and Association for Educational Communications and Technology. Reprinted by permission of the American Library Association. The Big6 Skills are used and adapted with permission. The Big6™ is copyright ©1987 Michael Eisenberg and Robert E. Berkowitz.

Note. Standards in boldface type apply specifically to the Giant Step on that page of the chart.

Giant Step #6	Information Literacy Standards	The Big6 Skills	Language Arts (High School)
Web Site Evaluation Get JUFTED!	**Information Literacy (Standard 1)**	**1. Task Definition**	**Standard 1: Vocabulary Development**
	Information Literacy (Standard 2)		**Standard 2: Reading—Comprehension**
	Information Literacy (Standard 3)	**2. Information Seeking Strategies**	Standard 3: Reading—Literary Response
	Independent Learning (Standard 4)	**3. Location and Access**	**Standard 4: Writing—Process**
	Independent Learning (Standard 5)	**4. Use of Information**	**Standard 5: Writing—Applications**
	Independent Learning (Standard 6)	**5. Synthesis**	**Standard 6: English Language Conventions (Grammar)**
	Social Responsibility (Standard 7)	**6. Evaluation**	Standard 7: Listening & Speaking
	Social Responsibility (Standard 8)		
	Social Responsibility (Standard 9)		

Survival Tool 10. Standards Chart

Excerpted from Chapter 2, "The Information Literacy Standards for Student Learning," of *Information Power: Building Partnerships for Learning*, by American Association of School Librarians and Association for Educational Communications and Technology. Copyright ©1998 American Library Association and Association for Educational Communications and Technology. Reprinted by permission of the American Library Association. The Big6 Skills are used and adapted with permission. The Big6™ is copyright ©1987 Michael Eisenberg and Robert E. Berkowitz.

Note: Standards in boldface type apply specifically to the Giant Step on that page of the chart.

Giant Step # 7	Information Literacy Standards	The Big6 Skills	Language Arts (High School)
Using Online Encyclopedias: World Book Online	**Information Literacy (Standard 1)**	**1. Task Definition**	Standard 1: Vocabulary Development
	Information Literacy (Standard 2)		**Standard 2: Reading— Comprehension**
	Information Literacy (Standard 3)	**2. Information Seeking Strategies**	Standard 3: Reading—Literary Response
	Independent Learning (Standard 4)	**3. Location and Access**	Standard 4: Writing—Process
	Independent Learning (Standard 5)	**4. Use of Information**	Standard 5: Writing— Applications
	Independent Learning (Standard 6)		Standard 6: English Language Conventions (Grammar)
	Social Responsibility (Standard 7)	5. Synthesis	Standard 7: Listening & Speaking
	Social Responsibility (Standard 8)	6. Evaluation	
	Social Responsibility (Standard 9)		

Survival Tool 10. Standards Chart

Excerpted from Chapter 2, "The Information Literacy Standards for Student Learning," of *Information Power: Building Partnerships for Learning*, by American Association of School Librarians and Association for Educational Communications and Technology. Copyright ©1998 American Library Association and Association for Educational Communications and Technology. Reprinted by permission of the American Library Association. The Big6 Skills are used and adapted with permission. The Big6™ is copyright ©1987 Michael Eisenberg and Robert E. Berkowitz.

Note: Standards in boldface type apply specifically to the Giant Step on that page of the chart.

Giant Step # ∞	Information Literacy Standards	The Big6 Skills	Language Arts (High School)
Don't Copy—Right?!?	**Information Literacy (Standard 1)**	1. Task Definition	**Standard 1: Vocabulary Development**
	Information Literacy (Standard 2)		**Standard 2: Reading—Comprehension**
	Information Literacy (Standard 3)	2. Information Seeking Strategies	**Standard 3: Reading—Literary Response**
	Independent Learning (Standard 4)	3. Location and Access	**Standard 4: Writing—Process**
	Independent Learning (Standard 5)	4. Use of Information	**Standard 5: Writing—Applications**
	Independent Learning (Standard 6)	5. Synthesis	**Standard 6: English Language Conventions (Grammar)**
	Social Responsibility (Standard 7)	6. Evaluation	**Standard 7: Listening & Speaking**
	Social Responsibility (Standard 8)		
	Social Responsibility (Standard 9)		

Survival Tool 10. Standards Chart

Excerpted from Chapter 2, "The Information Literacy Standards for Student Learning," of *Information Power: Building Partnerships for Learning*, by American Association of School Librarians and Association for Educational Communications and Technology. Copyright ©1998 American Library Association and Association for Educational Communications and Technology. Reprinted by permission of the American Library Association. The Big6 Skills are used and adapted with permission. The Big6™ is copyright ©1987 Michael Eisenberg and Robert E. Berkowitz.

Note. Standards in boldface type apply specifically to the Giant Step on that page of the chart.

Giant Step # 9	Information Literacy Standards	The Big6 Skills	Language Arts (High School)
AUPs	**Information Literacy (Standard 1)**	**1. Task Definition**	**Standard 1: Vocabulary Development**
	Information Literacy (Standard 2)	**2. Information Seeking Strategies**	**Standard 2: Reading— Comprehension**
	Information Literacy (Standard 3)		Standard 3: Reading—Literary Response
	Independent Learning (Standard 4)	**3. Location and Access**	Standard 4: Writing—Process
	Independent Learning (Standard 5)	**4. Use of Information**	Standard 5: Writing— Applications
	Independent Learning (Standard 6)		Standard 6: English Language Conventions (Grammar)
	Social Responsibility (Standard 7)	**5. Synthesis**	Standard 7: Listening & Speaking
	Social Responsibility (Standard 8)		
	Social Responsibility (Standard 9)	6. Evaluation	

Survival Tool 10. Standards Chart

Excerpted from Chapter 2, "The Information Literacy Standards for Student Learning," of *Information Power: Building Partnerships for Learning*, by American Association of School Librarians and Association for Educational Communications and Technology. Copyright ©1998 American Library Association and Association for Educational Communications and Technology. Reprinted by permission of the American Library Association. The Big6 Skills are used and adapted with permission. The Big6™ is copyright ©1987 Michael Eisenberg and Robert E. Berkowitz.

Note: Standards in boldface type apply specifically to the Giant Step on that page of the chart.

Information Literacy Standards	The Big6 Skills	Language Arts (High School)
Information Literacy (Standard 1)	**1. Task Definition**	Standard 1: Vocabulary Development
Information Literacy (Standard 2)	**2. Information Seeking Strategies**	Standard 2: Reading—Comprehension
Information Literacy (Standard 3)		Standard 3: Reading—Literary Response
Independent Learning (Standard 4)	**3. Location and Access**	Standard 4: Writing—Process
Independent Learning (Standard 5)	**4. Use of Information**	Standard 5: Writing—Applications
Independent Learning (Standard 6)	5. Synthesis	Standard 6: English Language Conventions (Grammar)
Social Responsibility (Standard 7)	**6. Evaluation**	Standard 7: Listening & Speaking
Social Responsibility (Standard 8)		
Social Responsibility (Standard 9)		

Survival Tool 10. Standards Chart

Excerpted from Chapter 2, "The Information Literacy Standards for Student Learning," of *Information Power: Building Partnerships for Learning*, by American Association of School Librarians and Association for Educational Communications and Technology. Copyright ©1998 American Library Association and Association for Educational Communications and Technology. Reprinted by permission of the American Library Association. The Big6 Skills are used and adapted with permission. The Big6™ is copyright ©1987 Michael Eisenberg and Robert E. Berkowitz.

Note: Standards in boldface type apply specifically to the Giant Step on that page of the chart.

Chapter 11

IMPLEMENT ONLINE COURSE

Survival Strategy

When reading the nine-page article in Giant Step 9 (the school's AUP or Acceptable Use Policy), make sure to highlight the main parts and SKIM! Do not read word-for-word. Otherwise, you will get bored and begin to lose focus on what you're reading.—Allison Tyler, BDHS Sophomore (**A great implementation strategy! Get feedback from students in the pilot and post it in the final project for others to benefit from! pb**)

Survival Strategy

When rating search engines, be sure to look at a Web site the engine turned up. This will help you to rate the usefulness of the sites retrieved. Also, don't base your rating on the number of hits retrieved, but rather on the validity of those hits.—Ben Jarvis, BDHS Sophomore (**Another great implementation strategy—by a student for a student! pb**)

When it comes to implementation of an online unit, my best advice to you is to start SMALL! After creating the unit, I started by collaborating with one teacher in order to try it out on a small scale. The "launching" of this first attempt was invaluable, however, and made the next step of the process much smoother sailing! The next step to consider for implementation is moving the unit to an entire grade level. This will give you the opportunity to work with a variety of teachers with different styles, opinions, and insights, as well as a variety of classes with varied needs. After reflection and refining of the unit with one grade level, you will be ready to tackle a "whole school" implementation project. At this time, you will have had a chance to work the bugs out and the unit should have clear routines and procedures that will assist you with the implementation steps.

Another piece of advice: be flexible! Online instruction is unique in that you cannot react to students as easily or normally as you would in a regular classroom. Questions pertaining to online assignments and information are delayed with e-mail. As students work through the material independently, they may come to a point where teacher intervention is required. Teacher responses may not come as quickly as students—or their parents—would like (a barrier mentioned in chapter 2). All barriers should be addressed to smooth out the rough edges during implementation. Not to worry, though, smooth sailing will soon take place!

We have also found that it is important to work with your administrators, department chairs, and lead teachers to ensure that all stakeholders buy in to the process. That way, it's not just the media specialist's implementation of the plan, but the entire team's goal. At our school, this online unit is critical in helping to meet the School Improvement Team goal of increased reading comprehension skills and ensures a clear connection between the media center and the classrooms.

Implement Online Course

I see a valuable connection between implementation and evaluation, specifically formative evaluation. It is important to realize that course development is never done. Online teachers can never say that they have "finished" creating a course. Not only does technology continually change and improve methods of online instruction, but students and even the information that we teach change on a regular basis. Online learning is a fluid system that reacts and flows according to present and even future trends. As an online teacher, make sure to move with the flow and remember that the online environment is very different from a regular classroom.

Survival Tips: Start SMALL!

S   Seek help and "buy-in" from administrators, department chairs, and lead teachers for establishing an implementation plan.

M   Make improvements to the unit along the way. Start small during the first pilot and slowly build up to the full implementation.

A   Assess student progress often and provide the results to the various stakeholders for ongoing reflection to make any needed implementation changes.

L   Listen to suggestions! (Refer to chapter 8.) and look carefully at feedback (Survival Tool 11b). Are you getting the right feedback?

L   Leave it alone for a few days. Rather than make constant changes, give the unit a rest. After your break, you'll be more objective and have an easier time seeing what changes need to be made.

Post information often during implementation

Survival Source 11

http://ncsdWeb.ncsd.k12.wy.us/dherman/Lesley/week2/lesson/lesson_rubric.html

This site provides an example of a rubric that could be used for teacher self-reflection *after* lesson implementation. It could also be easily used *before* the lesson to ensure critical components, like library standards and course content, are covered.

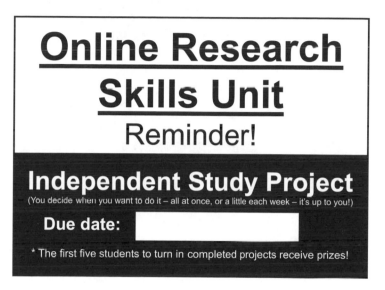

Survival Tool 11a. Research Unit Reminders

"Capture the Giant" Online Orientation Discussion Board Example

Survival Tool 11b. Discussion Boards

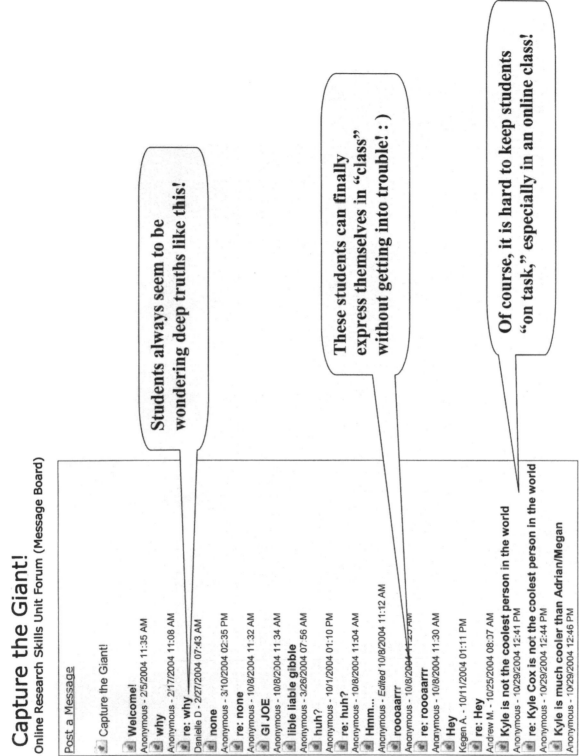

Survival Tool 11b. Discussion Boards

Chapter 12

DATA, DATA, DATA!

Survival Strategy

The SRI test is extremely easy. I have taken this exact same test every year since first grade and my results have remained consistent for the last six years. I believe taking this inventory is a waste of time that could be put to better use learning something of educational value!—Mary Jenkins, BDHS Senior **(Use data to determine who can "test out!" pb)**

Is being data-driven "driving" you crazy? I understand how overwhelming it can be deciding what data to collect, how to best collect them, and once you have the information, what to do with it. I have found that we often tend to collect too much information and need to begin with the end in mind. What do we want students to know and be able to do at the end of our online unit? What specifically will that look like in the media center? With that vision in mind, what has to be measured? What data do we need to collect to be sure that we are working toward that vision? "Who?" is also a question to ask (all, specific classes, specific types of students). The process that I have found most helpful is to first collect data on which classrooms are accessing the online unit and completing the tasks. Those data can be collected on a simple dated checklist either on your computer spreadsheet or on a hard copy included with your plans and schedules in your binder.

Once you know which classrooms have completed the unit, you can take the next step to collect data on whether—or not—students are now able to independently use the media center to access resources and complete research. While this may be hard to document, it is extremely valuable. Using a rubric to measure classroom success is another survival tip. (See Survival Tool 12.) The tool to assist you in developing your own individual rubrics is Rubistar (http://www.rubistar.com).

In our media center, we keep a checklist of which classrooms sign up for the library and have a way to quickly log whether the students and teacher require support—or if they only require facilitation from us to complete their tasks. In addition, these data can be compared to classes that have not completed the online unit in order to show the value of the skills gained from the lessons. We then can tally the results to determine whether the unit has been effective (see example below). Another example of data use that is extremely helpful is including this information along with library usage in the annual report. There is evidence that there is a direct link between students and teachers using the library resources more frequently after they have completed the unit and are familiar with how to access the materials they need in a quick and efficient manner.

Data: What to Collect? What Does It Mean?

Another place where a plan is necessary! As educators, we are all about the business of student achievement. Even though the collection of data is time-consuming, it is critical. Data should be posted for teachers, administrators, students, and even parents to see. One question also should be asked, "Which comes first, the data or the evaluation?" The two actually go together in that data are part of the evaluation and can be used to show success and the value of a well-developed program.

Survival Tips: Data Decisions

D   Decide on the necessary data to be collected to make future decisions and improvements to the content.

A   Analyze your data to make program improvements.

T   Tell others about the results of your data collection in order to validate the importance of your project.

A   Ask for help! Don't be afraid to ask others with more experience on data collection for suggestions on formatting your data and ideas for time-management strategies.

Survival Source 12

http://depts.washington.edu/oeaias/

The IAS (Instructional Assessment System) online site includes sample data collection forms and sample reports that could be modified for your own data collection needs. View a demo and, if funds are available, find out rates for IAS to create a custom database for your number-crunching needs. You can "count" on this site to make data decisions easier!

"Capture the Giant" Online Orientation
Classroom Evaluation Form

Teacher: _____

Period(s): _____

Semester: _____

Year: _____

Date online unit completed: _____

Library Sign-Up Log

Date	Requests/Project	Worked Independently	Tally of Help needed

Comments:

Survival Tool 12. Data Decisions

Chapter 13

EVALUATE

Survival Strategy

I feel this activity really orients you with the different aspects of the library. I didn't think I was a great library-oriented person, but after evaluating my performance, I think this program has been very useful to me.—Matt Carter, BDHS Sophomore **(Self-evaluation! Yippee! pb)**

An ongoing theme throughout this book has been the importance of reflective evaluation, utilizing both formal and informal means to determine the effectiveness of your project. The importance of assessment simply cannot be overlooked. At this time, our focus is more global, evaluating not only this online unit but also the effectiveness of online courses as a whole. With the important role that technology plays in our society, it is vital that teachers find ways to integrate technology into the instructional process in a way that facilitates learning and saves time for both the student and the instructor.

Evaluation provides the answers that we need to make important instructional decisions such as: Was this lesson or unit effective in meeting the objectives? Were the standards mastered? Do data show that this unit was effective in meeting student learning and behavioral goals? If the answers are yes, then the online unit was effective! If not, it is time to rethink the process after reflecting on the evaluation data.

One of the changes we are evaluating right now is whether it is time to go paperless. Basically, we're evaluating whether or not students should really need to print out projects. While some students (like me!) find security in printing out their work, being paperless and folderless would streamline the process. But are we ready to take that GIANT step yet? We'll see!

Evaluate

> Dr. Elizabeth Oyer of Evaluation Solutions has been involved with IOA as an outside evaluator. Her philosophy points to the fact that "the most appropriate, valid approach to evaluation emerges from the goals and objectives of the project, intervention or curriculum." She also mentioned in a recent conversation that measuring the value of online education in terms of cost, satisfaction, and student achievement is the primary function of an evaluation. Is online instruction paying benefits? How does the quality of an online course compare to regular class instruction? These are all points to consider in the evaluation stage.

Keep in mind, it's important not only to measure the learning outcomes of students (see Survival Tools 13a and 13b), but also, as stated earlier, to collect their input on both their learning and instruction. IOA uses a student survey at the end of each semester to collect these data. Students respond to questions focused on the organization of the content, teaching approaches, and timely feedback, as well as the interaction with and ability to contact teachers.

The best student feedback is actually collected when students are asked the following informal questions:

1. Would you recommend an online course to your friends? (The answer to this question says a lot about the student's experience.)

2. What is/was the single best aspect of this course? (Another avenue to great feedback!)

3. What would you like to see changed in this online course?

The responses to these questions can be utilized by teachers not only to continually improve the content but also to refine instructions. Online teachers can also take advantage of the questions that students ask as they progress through the online content. These questions usually arise from weak areas that may need more explanation, clarity, or detail.

Furthermore, it is important to remember that evaluation is ongoing and you are never finished evaluating—even after several positive evaluations! I once read that if you aren't changing, then you aren't growing. In essence, evaluation is a cyclical process, forcing you to evaluate changes that have been made from previous evaluations. Evaluation tools assist us by ensuring that the changes we are making are based on solid reflection data, rather than just "changing with the tide!"

We hope that this SURVIVAL GUIDE will help you to have a successful online unit with "smooth sailing!"

Survival Tips: AHOY!

A   Actively pursue evaluation at every opportunity (evaluation should be ongoing).

H   Have a variety of evaluation procedures, both formal and informal.

O   Optimize your time! Utilize the survey tools in available online courseware whenever possible to make evaluation easier.

Y   YAHOO! Make sure to celebrate the small steps! Ongoing courses take time to implement successfully!

Ahoy, mates! You've completed the SURVIVAL GUIDE and are now ready to set sail into the online orientation. With the electronic version, you can modify the unit for your individual needs—and dive right into the pilot project!

Survival Source 13

http://www.remc.11.k12.mi.us/bcisd/classres/restch.htm

This site is invaluable after you have evaluated your course and are ready to refine or research areas for improvement or extension.

ONLINE COURSE EVALUATION

1. I was able to navigate through the online unit easily.   Y   S   N

    Comments:

2. The online unit was interesting and helpful.   Y   S   N

    Comments:

3. I could get help from my instructor when needed.   Y   S   N

    Comments:

4. I was able to interact with my classmates as needed.   Y   S   N

    Comments:

5. The online unit was relevant to me and my needs.   Y   S   N

    Comments:

6. I would recommend continuing with this online unit.   Y   S   N

    Comments:

****

Overall Comments:

Key:
Y—Yes
S—Sometimes
N—No

Survival Tool 13a. Online Course Evaluation

ONLINE INSTRUCTOR EVALUATION

1. The instructor was well prepared.   Y   S   N

   Comments:

2. The instructor provided individual help as needed.   Y   S   N

   Comments:

3. The instructor included real-world learning in this unit.   Y   S   N

   Comments:

4. The instructor answered my questions effectively.   Y   S   N

   Comments:

5. The instructor was accessible to me and the class.   Y   S   N

   Comments:

6. I received prompt feedback on my grades/scores.   Y   S   N

   Comments:

****

Overall Comments:

Key:
Y—Yes
S—Sometimes
N—No

Survival Tool 13b. Online Instructor Evaluation

Part II

"CAPTURE THE GIANT:"
ONLINE RESEARCH SKILLS UNIT

MEDIA CENTER ONLINE ORIENTATION

Sophomore Scavenger Hunt: Capture the Giant!

Introduction

YOUR HELP IS DESPERATELY NEEDED! An evil Giant is lurking somewhere in the shadowy, crowded halls of **[INSERT YOUR SCHOOL NAME HERE!]**, threatening to destroy any and all information he can find. You won't see this Giant (although you may feel his presence at times), but he can see you! Tired of being called names for being academically challenged, he wants every student to be in the dark as well. He thinks that if he keeps the keys of knowledge to himself, he will, at last, be the smartest Giant in the building and, maybe soon, the entire world!

The Giant's mission: to cheat you out of important lifelong learning skills. We wouldn't want that, now would we? The only way to prevent the Giant from accomplishing his goal is to take Giant steps to beat him at his own game. You'll race the Giant to the finish and, if you succeed, will win information literacy skills, not only for you, but for the entire student body here at **[INSERT YOUR SCHOOL HERE]** and (who knows) maybe even the universe! Oh, no!

NOTES

[INSERT YOUR NAME HERE!]

Your librarian is counting on you to save the media center from this same horrible fate! As part of his secret plan, the Giant hopes to destroy each and every book in our Media Center. A school without books? Oh no! To assist you on your journey to beat the Giant, your media specialist and teacher will be providing help for you as you stumble along the darkened path toward the light of knowledge. Anytime you see text <u>that is underscored,</u> they are providing examples and/or help to you.

For your journey, you will need to gather some supplies. Your GIANT SURVIVAL KIT should include:

- Library Research Pocket Folder

- Pencil or Pen

- Computer with Internet Access

- Printer

The Rules

- You must take each Giant step in order.

- You must master each step before taking the next step.

- Remember: Put your best foot forward at all times!

- After you take all ten steps, you must still complete one last Giant step successfully to end your journey.

The Task

Your fellow students, who are not nearly as experienced and competent, are counting on you. Some have taken Giant steps and are near the end of the mission; others have not yet begun their journey. In some of the Giant steps, you will work with your fellow students to accomplish the tasks. Most of the steps, however, require you to work alone—so that you can concentrate fully on the important job of saving the Information Age for all of us.

NOTES

Luckily for you, the Giant is a horrible typist and won't be able to keep up with your amazing word processing skills. Before taking your first step, *create a new Microsoft Word document.* On the heading of the document, type your name, date, English teacher's name, and period in the top left-hand corner of your document. Because you will be using this document throughout your journey, be sure to SAVE the document in the following format: LAST NAME-library-05. (For example, <u>SMITH-library-05</u>). Throughout your journey, you will be asked to record several of your answers in this document—so you may just want to minimize Word while you're working so that you can go back. If you run out of time, just save your project as directed above and you can access it when you return to the project.

NOTES

GIANT STEP 1A: Locating Books in the Online Card Catalog

(Big6 Skills: 1. Task Definition; 2. Information Seeking Strategies; and 3. Location and Access).

Think About It!

When was the last time you checked out a library book? For some of you, I bet it's been since grade school. We're glad you're back!

Directions:

1. Go to a media center online card catalog. **[PROVIDE DIRECTIONS FOR STUDENTS HERE. WHERE IS YOUR BOOK SEARCH COMPUTER LOCATED?]**

2. Perform a keyword search under a subject you are interested in. (for example, "football" or "romance").

3. Write down the call number. If the call number contains an "F" or "FIC," the book is fiction. If the call number contains a number, the book is nonfiction. (Nonfiction books are organized by the Dewey Decimal Classification System. No matter what library you go into, all nonfiction books are organized the same way.)

SPINE LABEL WITH CALL NUMBER

4. Locate this book (or another one you have found) and check it out. Open your Word document and type a note to your librarian about what book you checked out and why you chose this particular book. Include the author, title, and call number. Be sure to include the date you checked out this book—and the date the book is due.

    (Example: Today (August 1, 2003) I checked out the book *Holes* by Louis Sachar (F SAC). I wanted to read this book because I saw the movie this summer and it was really good. The book is due in two weeks—on August 14, 2000).

5. Next, perform a title search for the book *The Call of the Wild* by Jack London. Write down the call number.

6. Find the book on the shelf and type the barcode of this book in your Word document. (Example: Barcode 300086127).

NOTES

BARCODE NUMBER

7.   Finally, perform a keyword search under your favorite author. How many books does the library have by the author? Enter the information in your Word document. <u>(Example: I really like books by Caroline Cooney. I searched under her name and found that our media center has 22 Cooney books.)</u>

Note: If the media center computers are full, you can perform a book search from any school computer by going to: **[INSERT HTTP ADDRESS HERE].**

NOTES

GIANT STEP 1B: Book Quiz

Read a book of your choice (or one assigned by your English teacher!) and take a quiz about your book. See your librarian for instructions when you are ready.

Congratulations! You have successfully completed the Giant Step 1 challenge and are ready to move forward. If you think you're ready for another challenge, go on to Giant Step 2 now. You'd better hurry, though, because the Giant is one step ahead of you!

NOTES

GIANT STEP 2: Searching the Library Database

(Big6 Skills: 1. Task Definition; 2. Information Seeking Strategies; 3. Location and Access; and 4. Use of Information).

Think About It!

What is a database? Why might it be better than the "generic" Internet for research?

Directions:

1. Log on to any media center computer.

2. From the desktop, click on the library research database.

3. When the database loads, enter the name of a person you are researching for English class. If you aren't currently researching a person (author, inventor, etc.), then type in the name of someone famous you would like to learn more about.

4. Open your Microsoft Word document and list three bulleted facts about the person. Example:

   Michael Jordan
   - Jordan was born on February 17, 1963 in New York.
   - Jordan was cut from the baseball team in high school.
   - Jordan earns more money for endorsements than playing basketball.

5. Now that you've researched the database for a person, choose a topic you are researching for your English teacher (or a topic of interest).

6. Scan through the articles until you see a specific title that sounds like it would fit the type of article you need (Example: If you are looking for information about Stephen King, then you probably want a biographical article—not a book review for *The Green Mile*).

7. Click on the chosen article and read it.

8. Open your Word document and type a 3–5 sentence summary of the article. *Please include the article's title, author, section, and page number on which it appeared.*

9. Next, open your Word document and type the citation information for each article. You can then simply cut and paste the citations into your Works Cited page later. (Example: "**The Dust Bowl, 1934–1938.**" *DISCovering U.S. History*. Gale Research, 1997. Reproduced in History Resource Center. Farmington Hills, MI: Gale Group. http://galenet.galegroup.com/servlet/HistRC/).

Great job! You have mastered Giant Step 2. The good news is that this step was the hardest and longest part of your mission. The bad news is that the journey isn't over yet! You are currently tied with the Giant—he's looking over your shoulder right now, trying to steal your answers. Watch out! To go on to the next step, click on Giant Step 3.

NOTES

GIANT STEP 3: Out of "Cite!"

Think About It!

When was the last time you had to do a Works Cited page? Was it like pulling teeth? Well, not to worry! There's a new technology tool that makes citing sources "out of cite!"

This Giant step shows you how to use a Web tool to help you make your next Works Cited page! No need to worry about what's underlined, where the comma goes, if the author's last name is first . . . it's all done for you! With this amazing tool, you'll be way ahead of the Giant!

Directions:

1. Log on to any Internet-accessible computer.

2. Go to the Internet.

3. Open the following link: http://www.landmarkproject.com/citation_machine/index.php

4. Click on "Book" (found in the left-hand yellow column under "Print Resources").

5. Enter the citation information for the book you checked out in Giant Step 1. (Fill in all the blanks! If you can't find something, leave it blank!)

6. Click on "Make Citation." Voila! Like magic, your source is put in perfect Works Cited format! How great is that?

7. All you need to do now is copy and paste the MLA citation into your Word document. It's that easy!

Giant Step 4 is a task that you will complete outside the school building. No, you don't get to leave school during the day—darn it! You do, however, get a magical card that will allow you to have millions and millions of books, videos, and even CDs! To get your magic card, go on to Giant Step 4.

NOTES

GIANT STEP 4: Get Carded—At Your Public Library!

Think About It!

Is your public library card gathering dust? Don't have one? Now's your chance to get carded—at your nearby Public Library!

1. If you don't already have a Public Library card, this step requires you to get a card.

2. You will need to go to the nearest branch of your Public Library (or any branch that is convenient for you) and complete an application.

3. When you go to get your card, make sure to take an ID (driver's license or other picture ID that includes your address).

4. The Public Library's address is: _____.

5. To find all about how many materials you can check out at a time and all the different types of materials available, go to: **[INSERT HTTP ADDRESS HERE]**.

6. The Public Library is open the following hours:

   Monday–Thursday _____
   Friday   _____
   Saturday   _____
   Sunday   _____

7. After you have gotten your public library card, place a copy of the card in your Library Research Folder.

NOTES

GIANT STEP 5: Online Searching

Think About It!

Which search engine do you regularly use? Why do you use it instead of another one?

Directions:

1. Fill in the following chart to practice your search skills on the Web.

2. After you complete the chart, copy and paste the chart into your Word document.

3. List other search engines you could have used and paste the list into your Word document.

Search Engine Used	Google www.google.com	Yahoo www.yahoo.com	Dogpile www.dogpile.com
Search Terms Used			
Number of Hits			

Congratulations! The good news is that you successfully completed Giant Step 5! The bad news is that the Giant noticed you were a bit distracted during the last step and took advantage of the situation to move ahead. In fact, you've been feeling distracted quite a bit lately, but don't want to give up the challenge—or let the Giant overhear you. You decide to search the Web for a trustworthy Question & Answer site that might be able to tell you why your concentration is off. Luckily, the person (or Giant) on the computer for you was at a perfect site to provide answers. You sit down and see the health site named "Go Ask Alice." You know you can't depend on just any Internet site to get answers, so you have to check it out first.

Go Ask Alice home page: http://www.goaskalice.columbia.edu

NOTES

GIANT STEP 6: Web Site Evaluation

Think About It!

Do you think you're a pretty good Internet surfer? Well, we're "juft" gonna have to find out!

Get JUFTED!

Get what? Get JUFTED! You mean you've never heard of it before? Well, to those who "juft" got here, JUFTED is the way to decide whether or not an Internet site is a good source. As you know, anyone (even a dumb Giant!) can put information on the Internet—after all, it's not rocket science. You want to know that the information you find is good! Here's how to use JUFTED:

J	Judgmental	Is the site judgmental (passes judgment) or objective (open-minded) about the information presented?
U	Up to Date	Is the information current and up-to-date or old, outdated? (Check the copyright date!)
F	Factual	Is the information factual and accurate?
T	Trustworthy	Can the information be trusted? Is the person who wrote it an authority (knowledgeable) on the subject? (Is the site sponsored by a college, hospital, or other reputable organization? Are the experts licensed in the medical or legal fields?)
E	Educational	Is the site educational and appropriate?
D	Detailed	Is enough detailed information provided? Does it cover all needed information—or is something important left out?

Note: Some of the JUFTED material only applies to educational research. For example, if you were an awesome skateboarder and interested in finding out about the latest stunts, you would want another skateboarder to share tips—probably not a doctor! Apply the JUFTED material to whatever kind of information you need for your topic.

You did it! Your outstanding evaluation of Internet sites put you ahead of the Giant—he's still trying to turn on the computer! There's still a chance for him to catch up with you, though, so keep on going!

NOTES

GIANT STEP 7: Using Online Encyclopedias: World Book Online

Think About It!

When did you first start using *World Book Encyclopedias*? Elementary school? Junior high? Well, they're still an awesome resource and a great starting point for research!

In order to beat the Giant at his own game, you're going to need to find out something about his background. Follow these steps for BIG success!

Directions:

1. Go to the World Book Online Encyclopedia at http://www.worldbookonline.com.

2. Enter the search term "Giant."

3. Read the article by Ellen J. Steckert.

4. Print out the article.

5. Next, find the *World Book Encyclopedia* (in print!) in the Media Center Reference section.

6. Write down the page on which the same article can be found in the offline (book) encyclopedia. (Write the page number on the top of your Giant article you just printed out.)

7. Place the printout in your Library Research Folder.

NOTES

GIANT STEP 8: Don't Copy—Right?!?

Think About It!

"No, it isn't murder. And as larceny goes, it's usually more distasteful than grand. But it is a bad thing, isn't it? Somehow we're never quite sure about plagiarism." This introductory paragraph to Thomas Mallon's book *Stolen Words* gives us something to think about.

You will now take your next Giant step—and discover how you feel about the "P" word!

Begin this activity by opening your Word document. Answer the following questions in a well-written, double-spaced paragraph. (**ALWAYS SAVE YOUR WORK FREQUENTLY!**)

What is plagiarism? Why is it wrong to plagiarize? Do you think some students plagiarize even though they don't mean to? What consequence should be given for students who are caught plagiarizing? Is there ever a time when it's okay to plagiarize?

Put your paragraph in your Library Research Folder.

Have you ever heard of TURNITIN.COM?

This is an awesome site (for teachers, anyway!). Anytime a teacher suspects a student of plagiarism (or that a paper might not be in a student's own words), he or she can turn in the paper to TURNITIN.COM. Even though librarians know a lot, turnitin is a lot quicker and more efficient than checking papers the old way!

The site then checks the student's paper against the Internet to see if there are any "direct matches." (In other words, has the paper been plagiarized?)

Now that you're done writing, spend some time researching plagiarism. Go to your favorite search engine and type in "Plagiarism in High School." Is it a problem—or not? What do you think? Discuss your answers with those sitting close to you.

Don't be one of these students. Always put your writing in your own words—not someone else's! That's plain, old cheating! Even "accidental" plagiarism has "GIANT" consequences at our school!

NOTES

GIANT STEP 9: AUPs

Think About It!

Why should schools have AUPs? Should your home have an AUP? What might be on it?

AUP stands for Acceptable Use Policy. When you "sign" an AUP, you are agreeing to abide by certain computer rules. Actually, you don't physically sign it—but it is an implied, understood policy for all students. The bottom line:

- EDUCATIONAL USE ONLY

- NO GAMES

- NO E-MAIL

- NO SURFING FOR NON-EDUCATIONAL USE!

Read the entire AUP here:

[POST YOUR AUP HERE OR PROVIDE THE HTTP ADDRESS.]

NOTES

GIANT STEP 10A: Exploring Your Media Center Web Site

Think About It!

Would you take an entire course (like English or social studies) online? Why or why not?

Did You Know?

Thanks to the Internet, you can get to our awesome Web site from anywhere by clicking on **[ENTER YOUR LIBRARY HOME PAGE ADDRESS HERE]**. You're now going to get a chance to explore our Web site to find the answers below. Who knows? You might even meet a familiar Giant along the way!

1. What are the hours your media center is open?

2. For easy reference, copy and paste (or type) the hours into your Word document.

3. Type the answers to the following true-false questions into your Word document.

    1. You can keep a library book for **[INSERT NUMBER HERE]** weeks.
    2. Students can borrow videos.
    3. Your library charges overdue fines.
    4. The media center is open for extended hours.
    5. Students can have food in the media center during lunch.
    6. Students can have soft drinks in the media center.
    7. Students can have water in the media center.
    8. Students must pay to use the copier.
    9. Students can borrow Reference books.
    10. Students can check out the most recent issues of magazines.
    11. Students cannot check out books if they have a book overdue.
    12. Students need a current ID to enter the media center.
    13. Students from study hall can visit the media center daily.
    14. Students can come to the media center during lunch without a pass.
    15. Students can always join the book club.

[NOTE: ANSWERS WILL VARY BASED ON YOUR OWN POLICIES AND PROCEDURES.]

4. Study and review the basic media center organization (fiction, nonfiction, reference, where these sections are located . . .). "Dewey" know the Dewey Decimal Numbers? You may want to review Giant Step 1 (the cyber Dewey site) before taking the Final Giant Step—your true test!

NOTES

GIANT STEP 10B: Putting It All Together!

First of all, a GIANT CONGRATULATIONS for completing the tasks and making it this far! In order to receive your "ticket for the test," and thus complete this tiring journey, you must now prepare your Library Research Folder:

1. Put all papers in correct order and LABEL all (Giant Step 1, Giant Step 2, Giant Step 3, and so on . . .).

2. Place all papers on the LEFT SIDE of your research folder.

3. Print out your completed Word document (LAST NAME-library-05).

4. Place the document on the RIGHT SIDE of your research folder.

5. Write your NAME, ENGLISH TEACHER, and ENGLISH PERIOD on the outside of your folder.

6. When your folder and all contents are in order, turn in your folder to your English teacher.

7. The folders will be graded and, if you "pass," you will receive your ticket to take the test.

NOTE: PLEASE FOLLOW ALL DIRECTIONS ABOVE. THE GIANT WILL REFUSE TO GRADE AND RETURN ALL FOLDERS THAT DO NOT MEET THE ABOVE CRITERIA!

Congratulations! You've now completed all ten steps and were successful in beating the Giant! The Information Age is safe for all students. All you have to do now is prove to your English teacher that you have successfully mastered the steps. When you are ready to test your knowledge, click here! Good luck!

FINAL STEP IN JOURNEY TO SAVE THE INFORMATION AGE!

GET YOUR TICKET TO TAKE THE ONLINE FINAL EXAM!

NOTES

Media Center Online Orientation Exam

1. What is your name?

2. Where can you access the library online card catalog?
   - ○ **A.** In the media center
   - ○ **B.** In the classroom
   - ○ **C.** At home
   - ○ **D.** In the lab
   - ○ **E.** All of the above

3. What information is critical to locating a book in the media center?
   - ○ **A.** Author's last name
   - ○ **B.** Title of book
   - ○ **C.** Call number
   - ○ **D.** Barcode number
   - ○ **E.** All of the above

4. What does the call number represent?
   - ○ **A.** Section and where in the section it can be found
   - ○ **B.** Section and author's first name
   - ○ **C.** Section and copyright date
   - ○ **D.** Section and the reserve status
   - ○ **E.** All of the above

5. Which of the following statements is false?
   - ○ **A.** Fiction books have numbers.
   - ○ **B.** Nonfiction books have numbers'
   - ○ **C.** Reference books are marked with an "R".
   - ○ **D.** Both a and b are false.

NOTES

6. If you're trying to find a book about bowling, you would search by:

   ○ **A.** Author

   ○ **B.** Title

   ○ **C.** Subject or keyword

   ○ **D.** Series

7. If your best friend says you absolutely must read *The Chocolate War*, you would search by:

   ○ **A.** Author

   ○ **B.** TItle

   ○ **C.** Subject or keyword

   ○ **D.** Series

8. If you're trying to find information about Tupac Shakur, you would search by:

   ○ **A.** Call numbers

   ○ **B.** Title

   ○ **C.** Subject or keyword

   ○ **D.** Series

9. You can access ilibrary from:

   ○ **A.** The media center

   ○ **B.** Home with a public library card

   ○ **C.** A school's computer lab

   ○ **D.** The Giant's cave (who has Internet access and a library card—Good Giant!)

   ○ **E.** All of the above

10. Which database category would you look in to find the best information on teen pregnancy?

    ○ **A.** Opposing Viewpoints/SIRS

    ○ **B.** Literature Resource Center

    ○ **C.** Oxford English Dictionary

    ○ **D.** History Resource Center

    ○ **E.** Biography Resource Center

NOTES

11. Which database will supply historical timelines?

   ○ **A.** Biography Resource Center

   ○ **B.** Business Resource Center

   ○ **C.** History Resource Center

   ○ **D.** Literature Resource Center

   ○ **E.** Famous People Resource Center

12. Which database area would be best to research Dell Computer Company?

   ○ **A.** Research

   ○ **B.** People

   ○ **C.** Business

   ○ **D.** Literature

   ○ **E.** Net Library

13. What is the correct way to access the periodical database?

   ○ **A.** Go directly to the database from the desktop.

   ○ **B.** Go to a search engine and type in database.

   ○ **C.** Click on the link from the media center Web site.

   ○ **D.** All of the above.

   ○ **E.** None of the above

14. You can e-mail database articles to your home to read or review later.

   ○ **A.** True

   ○ **B.** False

   ○ **C.** All of the above

   ○ **D.** None of the above

15. Why should you have (and use) a public library card?

   ○ **A.** The public library is open on nights and weekends.

   ○ **B.** The databases are always open to card members.

   ○ **C.** The public library has tons of materials that the school library does not have.

   ○ **D.** The public library has a variety of interesting programs.

   ○ **E.** All of the above.

NOTES

16. Where can you get a broad overview of a research topic before you begin?

   ○ **A.** World Book Online

   ○ **B.** Google

   ○ **C.** Go Ask Jeeves

   ○ **D.** Go Ask Alice

   ○ **E.** Yahoo

17. Which is the best place to search online?

   ○ **A.** Google

   ○ **B.** Yahoo

   ○ **C.** Inspire or ilibrary (or your specific magazine/periodical database)

   ○ **D.** Alta Vista

   ○ **E.** It depends on what you're looking for or what you find.

18. If you're looking for a trustworthy, valid, authoritative site, look mainly for those that end in:

   ○ **A.** .org

   ○ **B.** .edu

   ○ **C.** .gov

   ○ **D.** .com

   ○ **E.** a, b, and c

19. Online encyclopedias have the following advantages over print encyclopedias:

   ○ **A.** Video and audio/music streaming

   ○ **B.** More current, up-to-date information

   ○ **C.** Links to other sites

   ○ **D.** Volumes

   ○ **E.** A, B, and C

20. What might be the best way for a teacher to check a paper for plagiarism?

   ○ **A.** Submit paper to turnitin.com.

   ○ **B.** Ask the librarian.

   ○ **C.** Have the principal read the paper

   ○ **D.** Make an appointment with the Giant, who knows all.

NOTES

21. It is acceptable to use school computers to:

    ❍ **A.** Check personal e-mail if you don't stay on too long.

    ❍ **B.** Send a quick, instant message to the Giant.

    ❍ **C.** Shop for a prom dress.

    ❍ **D.** Check the ball scores.

    ❍ **E.** Research song lyrics for a poetry assignment.

22. Where is the nonfiction section?

    ❍ **A.** Front of the library

    ❍ **B.** Back of the library

    ❍ **C.** Library balcony

    ❍ **D.** Library reference room

    ❍ **E.** All of the above

23. Which of the following statements is false?

    ❍ **A.** Plagiarism is using someone else's work without permission.

    ❍ **B.** When you directly cite a source, you should use quotation marks.

    ❍ **C.** It's not plagiarism if you don't intend to cheat.

    ❍ **D.** Plagiarism occurs at our school.

24. An example of a person using a computer ethically is:

    ❍ **A.** A person who uses computer software to tutor a student.

    ❍ **B.** A person who prints song lyrics for a writing contest.

    ❍ **C.** A person who searches the Internet for family tree information.

    ❍ **D.** A person who reads the news each morning on CNN.com.

    ❍ **E.** All of the above.

NOTES

25. You would probably not want to use a Web site if it contained:

   ○ **A.** Judgmental information

   ○ **B.** Current information

   ○ **C.** Valid, truthful information

   ○ **D.** Information from a government or educational site

26. A book might be better than an Internet site for research if:

   ○ **A.** The Internet sites on a subject were blocked off.

   ○ **B.** The only Internet sites found were .com sites.

   ○ **C.** The book was outdated and directly related to your topic.

   ○ **D.** A and B only.

   ○ **E.** None of the above—the Internet is always the best choice.

NOTES

Media Center Online Orientation Exam Answer Key

1.	Varies	14.	A
2.	E	15.	E
3.	C	16.	A
4.	A	17.	E
5.	A	18.	E
6.	C	19.	E
7.	B	20.	A
8.	C	21.	E
9.	E	22.	B
10.	A	23.	C
11.	C	24.	E
12.	C	25.	A
13.	D (varies depending on setup)	26.	D

Part III

APPENDIXES

DEWEY WEBQUESTS

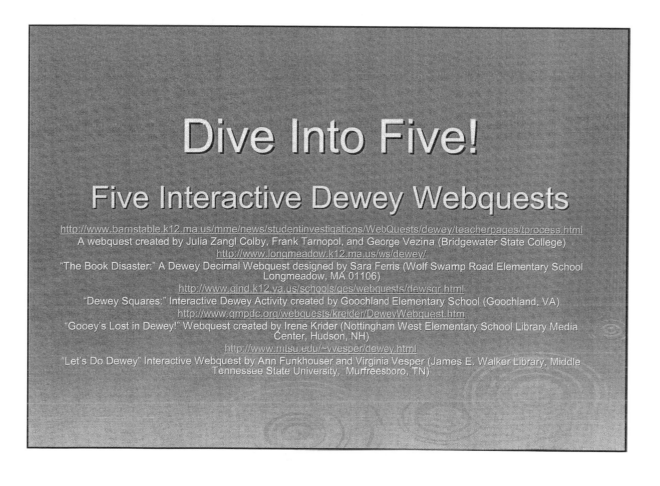

Dive Into Five!

Five Interactive Dewey Webquests

http://www.barnstable.k12.ma.us/mme/news/studentinvestigations/WebQuests/dewey/teacherpages/tprocess.html
A webquest created by Julia Zangl Colby, Frank Tarnopol, and George Vezina (Bridgewater State College)
http://www.longmeadow.k12.ma.us/ws/dewey/
"The Book Disaster:" A Dewey Decimal Webquest designed by Sara Ferris (Wolf Swamp Road Elementary School Longmeadow, MA 01106)
http://www.glnd.k12.va.us/schools/ges/webquests/dewsqr.html
"Dewey Squares:" Interactive Dewey Activity created by Goochland Elementary School (Goochland, VA)
http://www.gmpdc.org/webquests/kreider/DeweyWebquest.htm
"Gooey's Lost in Dewey!" Webquest created by Irene Krider (Nottingham West Elementary School Library Media Center, Hudson, NH)
http://www.mtsu.edu/~vvesper/dewey.html
"Let's Do Dewey" Interactive Webquest by Ann Funkhouser and Virginia Vesper (James E. Walker Library, Middle Tennessee State University, Murfreesboro, TN)

Appendix 2

INFORMATION LITERACY POWERPOINT PRESENTATION: YOUR "STANDARD" POWERPOINT

This PowerPoint presentation is great to have scrolling on your LCD—or simply select whichever slides (e.g., standards-based skills) you're working on that day.

Information Literacy Standards

The Standard Nine

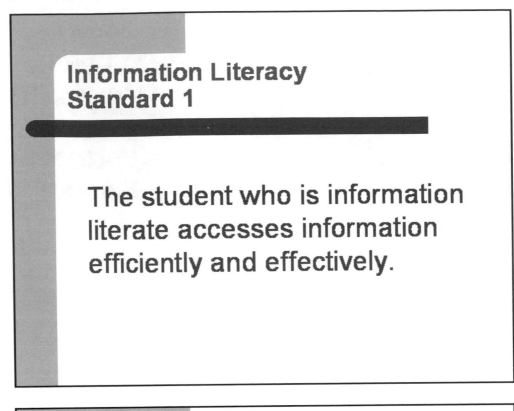

**Information Literacy
Standard 1**

The student who is information literate accesses information efficiently and effectively.

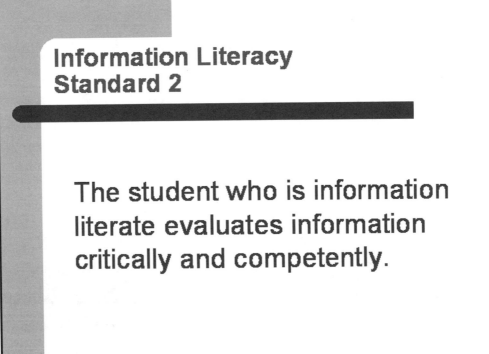

**Information Literacy
Standard 2**

The student who is information literate evaluates information critically and competently.

Information Literacy
Standard 3

The student who is information literate uses information accurately and creatively.

Independent Learning
Standard 4

The student who is an independent learner is information literate and pursues information related to personal interests.

Independent Learning
Standard 5

The student who is an independent learner is information literate and appreciates literature and other creative expressions of information.

Independent Learning
Standard 6

The student who is an independent learner is information literate and strives for excellence in information seeking and knowledge generation.

Social Responsibility
Standard 7

The student who contributes positively to the learning community and to society is information literate and recognizes the importance of information to a democratic society.

Social Responsibility
Standard 8

The student who contributes positively to the learning community and to society is information literate and practices ethical behavior in regard to information and information technology.

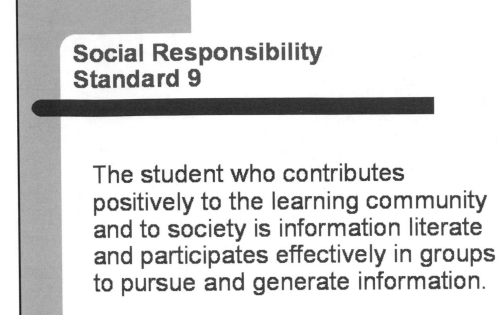

Social Responsibility
Standard 9

The student who contributes positively to the learning community and to society is information literate and participates effectively in groups to pursue and generate information.

Appendix 3

BAGWELL'S BEST:
ONLINE RESOURCES
FOR TEACHERS

Pam's research on the topic of online instruction led to many exceptional Survival Sources. I also spent some time looking and found a few more Web sites that provide a wealth of resources and experiences for the K–12 online learning audience.

http://vote.learn.unc.edu/bb/archives/cat_fully_online_courses.html
> Blackboard K–12 Users' Group (*Four Myths About Online Courses*)

http://www.shambles.net/elearning
> A comprehensive Web site with many online resources

http://www.sreb.org/programs/EdTech/toolkit/resources.asp
> The SREB Educational Technology Cooperative—This site leads to many others!

http://ts.mivu.org/default.asp?show=article&id=1059&action
> *Ten Ways Online Education Matches, or Surpasses, Face-to-Face Learning* (MIVU)

http://www.masie.com/701tips/
> *701 Tips for e-Learning* is a free digital book produced by The MASIE Center

http://www.ncrel.org/policy/pubs/html/pivol11/apr2002c.htm
> *Virtual Schools and E-Learning in K–12 Environments*—NCREL

http://www.nclbtechsummits.org/summit2/presentations/2.5.deFord_et_al.pdf
> *Developing e-Learning Content to Meet Learner Needs: Building versus Buying* (US DOE)

http://otel.uis.edu/
> Office of Technology—Enhanced Learning

RubiStar: http://rubistar.4teachers.org/index.php
> Create customized rubrics in English and Spanish.

http://www.e-learningguru.com/index.htm
> Practical information on e-learning in a plain-language format.

http://www.nacol.org/resources/
> North American Council for Online Learning

http://www.ncrel.org/tech/elearn/index.html
> E-Learning Knowledge Base—NCREL

http://www.fno.org/fnoindex.html
> *Educational Technology for Engaged Learning and Literacy*

Appendix 4

"I WILL SURVIVE" (ALIEN VIDEO CLIP)

This appendix contains a link to the most hilarious video clip ever! An alien, while singing Gloria Gaynor's "I Will Survive," gets crushed by a disco ball (you have to see it to get the idea!). I've shown the clip to students as a reminder to keep up with their online course before they are "crushed" by the deadline. I've also used the clip as an introduction to professional development workshops. As media specialists, we can survive anything! *Note:* Victor Navone production © 1999.

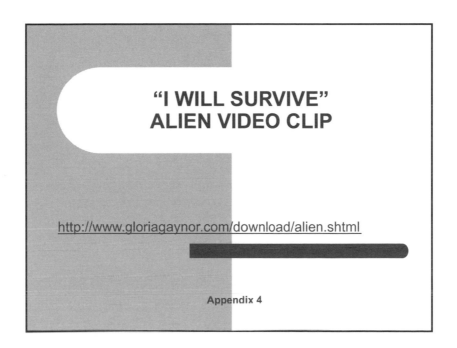

"I WILL SURVIVE"
ALIEN VIDEO CLIP

http://www.gloriagaynor.com/download/alien.shtml

Appendix 4

Appendix 5

COURSE OUTLINE:
GET A LITTLE
"INSPIRATION!"

This appendix is a course outline of the "Capture the Giant" Online Orientation in Inspiration format. If you haven't used Inspiration with your kids, maybe an example will "inspire" you to do so!

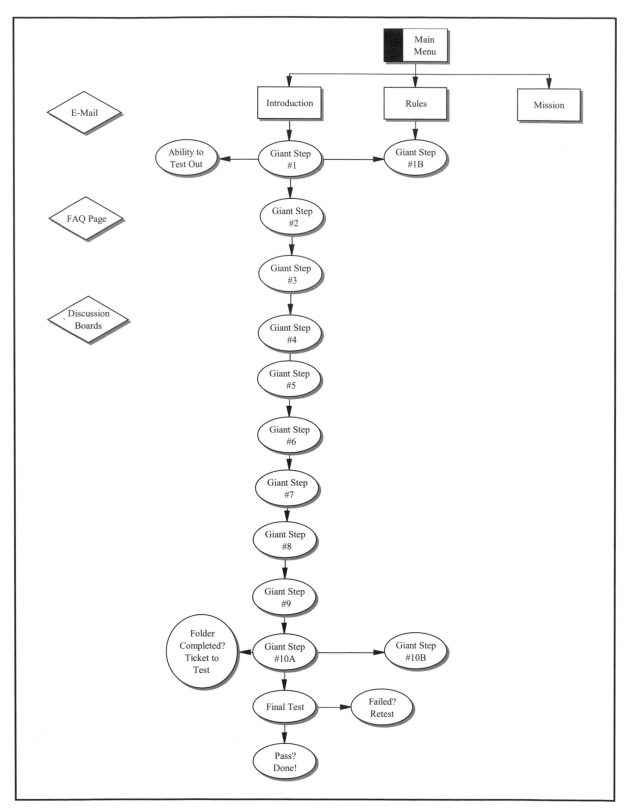

"Capture the Giant": Online Course Outline
Created By Kelly Rich, Online Instructor

Appendix 6

RICH'S REMINDERS

I asked Kelly Rich, one of our awesome online instructors, to prepare ten "survival" tips for using online activities. Kelly is also "rich" in ideas!

"Rich's Reminders": Top Ten Online Activity Reminders

1. Arrive early! Make sure the computers are working.

2. Survey your students! Assess their knowledge with the computer programs prior to lesson implementation.

3. Create Web links in advance! This makes the lesson user-friendly for students to access key sites and saves time.

4. Search your Web sites ahead of time! Be sure to use the same computer the students will be using.

5. Access student login information and temporary login information! This will help you to assist students who do not know their network identification or who have difficulties.

6. Design the assignment to allow for cooperative, as well as individual, work.

7. Plan for the worst! Create a back-up plan in case the server/Internet goes down.

8. Check the timing! Make sure the assignment can be finished within the allotted time, taking login and logoff time into consideration.

9. Plan ahead for expectations of students who may be absent.

10. Sign up early for lab time! Schedule your class or an additional day just in case—it is always easier to drop a day than to add a day.

By Kelly Rich, Online Instructor

Appendix 7

HELBLING'S HELPS

Online instructor Rachel Helbling shares ten helpful hints for teaching online. Need a little help? Here it is!

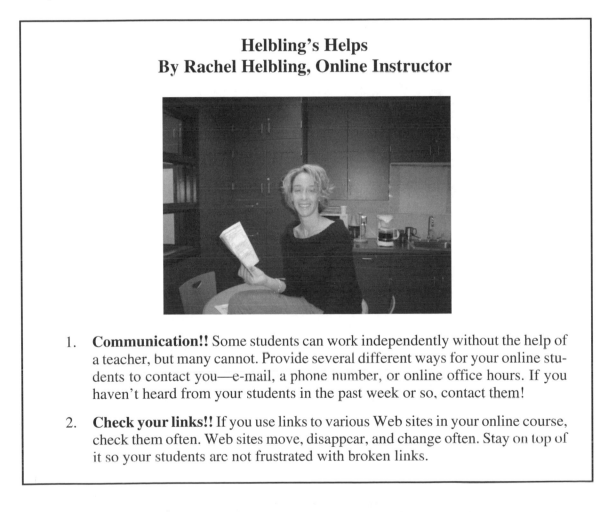

Helbling's Helps
By Rachel Helbling, Online Instructor

1. **Communication!!** Some students can work independently without the help of a teacher, but many cannot. Provide several different ways for your online students to contact you—e-mail, a phone number, or online office hours. If you haven't heard from your students in the past week or so, contact them!

2. **Check your links!!** If you use links to various Web sites in your online course, check them often. Web sites move, disappear, and change often. Stay on top of it so your students are not frustrated with broken links.

3. **Deadlines!!** One of the benefits of an online course is that students can work at their own pace—differentiation! However, this freedom can be difficult for many students as well. Posted, specific deadlines for assignments can help students pace themselves, and will allow you to monitor which students need a little bit of a push.

4. **Vary your assignments!!** It's easy to create an online course that consists entirely of "read-and-then-answer-the-questions" assignments. Students tend to get bored with this. By using the wide variety of resources available on the Internet, it is possible to provide your students with a number of different types of assignments. They can gather data to construct a graph or a table, make or solve a crossword puzzle, listen to a radio broadcast, or take a guided virtual field trip. The possibilities are virtually endless!

5. **Peer-to-Peer Communication!!** Some students are perfectly happy and productive operating completely independently. Creating opportunities for some peer-to-peer communication, however, is an important aspect for other students. Online discussions through monitored chat rooms or message boards are a good way to make students feel like they are part of a class. Students may also be encouraged to e-mail each other.

6. **Questions and Help!!** Make sure you are available for both! Although this is an online course, some students will have an easier time asking questions over the phone. Give students as many ways to contact you as possible—telephone office hours, online hours, posted hours in a chat room, or a "Help-me" message board that you check on a regular basis are some ideas that have worked well for me. If it is possible, some students will also benefit from a face-to-face meeting at some point near the beginning of the course. This will help them to feel more connected to you as a person instead of just a phantom voice on the other end of a phone line or a mysterious, faceless person on a computer.

7. **Organization!!** Textbooks are organized into Units, Chapters, and Sections. Students are familiar with this. Organizing your course online in a similar manner will help them to understand where they are in the course, what they have to complete, and what order they are supposed to complete it in. Posting a syllabus at the beginning of your course is a great way to give students a feel for how your course is organized. Since they are often being faced with the entire course at the beginning of a semester—it can be quite overwhelming. Having a way to break it down into smaller chucks can help with this feeling. As mentioned above, having deadlines for each small chunk of assignments can also help prevent students from feeling buried in course material.

8. **Visual!!** Put time into making the course environment and the assignments visually pleasing. Use graphics, photos, and videos of yourself teaching if possible. Make sure your directions are given in a format that is to the point and easy to read.

9. **Grades and Grading!!** Just like in a regular classroom-based class, students need to be aware of how they are progressing in the course . . . and because it's NOT a regular classroom-based course; students have an even more difficult time getting a feeling about how they are doing. Grade assignments in a timely fashion and make students' grades available to them as often as possible. Also, since students are working at their own pace in many online courses, assignments to be graded can pile up quickly—sometimes overnight. Frequent grading will help prevent the teacher from becoming overwhelmed with assignments as well.

10. **E-mail!!** This is something to be considered carefully. E-mail can be a wonderful way for students to feel a sense of camaraderie with other students in a course . . . but there are also issues that go along with it. Some students don't have access to e-mail, which can make them feel quite left out. Choosing an online learning environment that has a built-in e-mail system can eliminate this issue. Then there is the issue of cheating. There will always be those students who will try to e-mail answers and test questions to each other. Make sure to keep this possibility in mind when designing and monitoring your course.

SOPHOMORE SCAVENGER HUNT: AN ONLINE ACTIVITY

This scavenger-hunt activity was designed by students—for students—to use in an online setting. Searching for a great activity? No need for you to hunt any further—here it is!

Library Scavengers:

The Search for the LOST Books

by Joshua C.
BDHS Student

Step #1: Organize the Scavengers

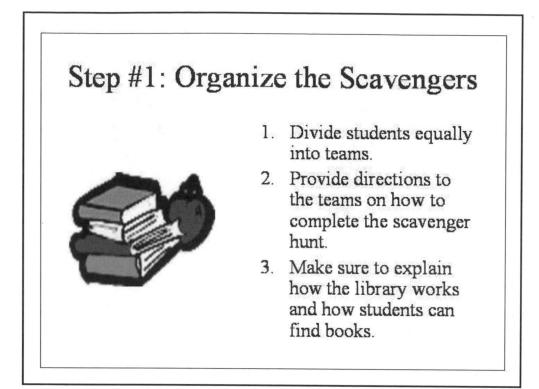

1. Divide students equally into teams.
2. Provide directions to the teams on how to complete the scavenger hunt.
3. Make sure to explain how the library works and how students can find books.

Step #2: What Are We Doing???

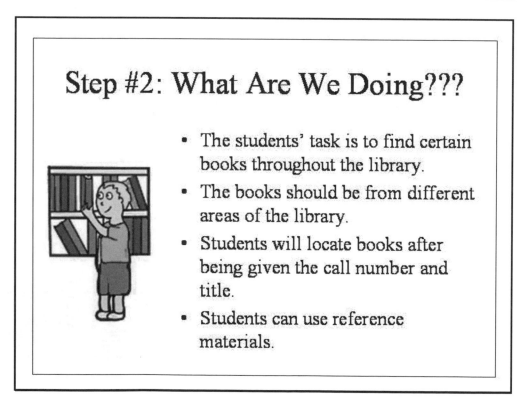

- The students' task is to find certain books throughout the library.
- The books should be from different areas of the library.
- Students will locate books after being given the call number and title.
- Students can use reference materials.

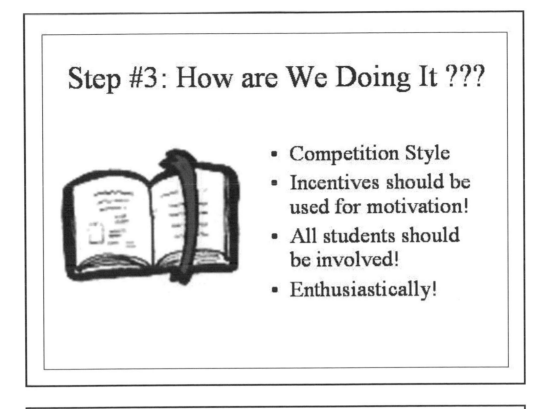

Step #3: How are We Doing It ???

- Competition Style
- Incentives should be used for motivation!
- All students should be involved!
- Enthusiastically!

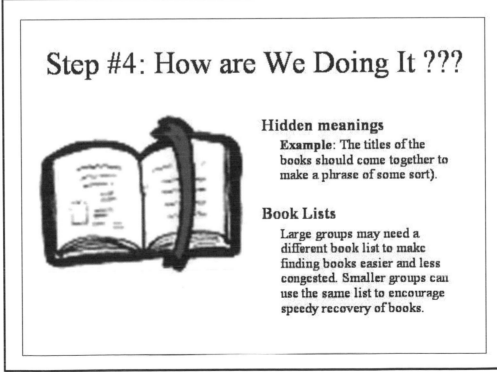

Step #4: How are We Doing It ???

Hidden meanings

    Example: The titles of the books should come together to make a phrase of some sort).

Book Lists

    Large groups may need a different book list to make finding books easier and less congested. Smaller groups can use the same list to encourage speedy recovery of books.

Step #5: Reward the Scavengers

- After the scavenger hunt, the winning team should be rewarded with the promised prizes.
- The teams that failed to complete their goals (or did not finish first) should be encouraged to do better the next time!

Notes:
- Ashley & Alicia helped Josh design this PowerPoint!
- All clip art is from www.clip-art.com and is copyright free!

Appendix 9

HIGH FIVE:
FIVE DI RESOURCES

Here are five outstanding links to differentiated instruction (DI) resources. Set sail for individualized instruction.

http://www.carelpress.co.uk/libraryskills.htm

"Check out" these great resources for differentiating library media center skills!

http://www.ascd.org/ed_topics/el200009_tomlinson.html

This article was written by one of the leading researchers in differentiation and is key to helping teachers understand the importance of differentiation.

http://home.nea.org/books/InspInd/chapter4.html

One of the keys to differentiation is for students to be able to work independently. This article gives specific strategies to teach students the skills needed to be able to work on their own. Yippee!

http://www.big6.com/showarticle.php?id=238

This article gives examples using a KWL chart, which can benefit students at all levels. The specific strategy of using different colors to categorize information (definitely a critical media center skill) is especially helpful for visual learners and lower level students. We know you'll want to learn about this strategy!

http://www.studygs.net/

This resource provides study guides and differentiation tools to meet the individual needs of students. You may even want to M.U.R.D.E.R. your students after checking out this site (not to worry . . . it's a strategy!).

Appendix 10

TWELVE SURVIVAL SLIDES

Dave and Libby "point" you in the right direction in this PowerPoint presentation focusing on online instruction.

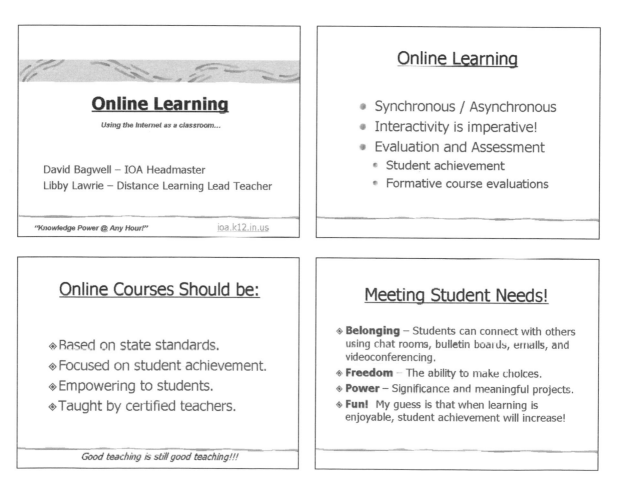

Online Learning

Using the Internet as a classroom...

David Bagwell – IOA Headmaster
Libby Lawrie – Distance Learning Lead Teacher

"Knowledge Power @ Any Hour!"   ioa.k12.in.us

Online Learning

- Synchronous / Asynchronous
- Interactivity is imperative!
- Evaluation and Assessment
  - Student achievement
  - Formative course evaluations

Online Courses Should be:

- Based on state standards.
- Focused on student achievement.
- Empowering to students.
- Taught by certified teachers.

Good teaching is still good teaching!!!

Meeting Student Needs!

- **Belonging** – Students can connect with others using chat rooms, bulletin boards, emails, and videoconferencing.
- **Freedom** – The ability to make choices.
- **Power** – Significance and meaningful projects.
- **Fun!** My guess is that when learning is enjoyable, student achievement will increase!

Courseware (ANGEL)

- An "easy tool" for course creation
- Enables interactive content
  - Chat
  - Whiteboard
  - E-mail
- Integrated Grading Tool
- Assessment Options

www.angellearning.com (ANGEL)

Course Structure vs. Flexibility

- Start / End dates (windows)
- Soft deadlines, target dates
- Extensions (INC Policy)

ONLINE LESSONS LEARNED

- Interactivity is Imperative! (Online courses should not be textbook based).
- Ongoing training for teachers is essential.
- Student success depends on prevention not reaction (regular feedback on lessons).
- Regular student contact via: email, phone, videoconferencing, or even face-to-face is critical.

Student Success

- GPA / Reading Skills
- Communication skills
- Students should be able to learn independently and need to be very self-motivated.

THE Success Story

"Thank you IOA, you changed directions for my life and opened doors that could have been closed to me forever!

Price of IOA if you do not live in the BD area......$300.00
Price of IOA if you do live in the BD area.............Free
Price of passing the final and getting your diploma... PRICELESS!"

Dustin W.

More Success Stories

- "Will I be able to take more of my classes online?"
- "It's 1:00am and I can't sleep! What a great time to do my work!" ☺
- "Do I really get credit for having this much fun?"

Assessment

- NCREL
  http://www.ncrel.org/sdrs/areas/as0cont.htm

- 4 Teachers.org
  http://www.4teachers.org
  - RubiStar
  - QuizStar

Online Textbooks

Prentice Hall
https://www.phsuccessnet.com/access/IPlanetServlet

Beyond Books
http://www.beyondbooks.com/

Holt
http://www.hrw.com/it/index.htm

DAVE'S TOP TEN SURVIVAL TIPS

No, he isn't David Letterman, but his top ten are great nevertheless!

1. **Update content continuously:** No online content should ever be considered finished. Improvements should be made on a regular basis in order for the course, lesson, or unit to be successful.

2. **Communicate frequently:** E-mail, phone, and speak with students directly if you can. This is necessary since the regular face-to-face instruction is usually not part of an online class.

3. **Grade regularly:** Students need frequent feedback to keep them motivated. Teachers can also get behind if they procrastinate!

4. **Use online resources:** Wow! There are literally thousands of resources out there for all to use on any topic.

5. **Be an expert:** Or at least know enough to answer student questions. Immerse yourself in the content and don't tackle subjects that you are not comfortable with.

6. **Broadband:** Good news, bad news. The bad news is that broadband costs more than basic dialup. The good news is that it is well worth the money. High speed Internet is also necessary for any hope of streaming educational videos that may be part of an on-line course.

7. **Who needs books!:** This is a little stab at Pam! I really believe that online content will become more and more prevalent as the years go by. . . . Look at what is happening to photography. Not that books will be obsolete, but online material will become more and more prevalent as time goes on.

8. **Schedule time (early or late):** Online office hours are another important need that replaces the regular classroom. This advice should also be given to students so that they work on their coursework regularly.

9. **Get others involved (chats):** Interactivity is the key to online instruction. Chatting and message boards (forums) should be used to enhance learning and get students to converse. Learning takes place when students share ideas and react to the ideas of others. Students who wouldn't dare speak in front of others in a typical class will sometimes share a great deal in the safety of an online environment.

10. **Last but not least, plan ahead (follow a schedule):** Students will typically procrastinate and not complete their work on time, if at all. Set times and target dates for work to be completed. You can be flexible with deadlines, but require students to be responsible if they miss any target. Make sure to use rewards and consequences!

REFERENCES

"CyberDewey." 1989. *CyberDewey.* Available at http://www.anthus.com/CyberDewey/CyberDewey.html (accessed January 16, 2005).

DiPetta, Tony, John M. Novak, and Zopito Marini. 2002. *Inviting Online Education.* 1st ed. Bloomington, IN: Phi Delta Kappa Educational.

Horton, Sarah. 2000. *Web Teaching Guide.* New Haven, CT: Yale University Press.

Iverson, Kathleen M. 2005. *E-Learning Games.* 1st ed. Upper Saddle River, NJ: Pearson Education.

Kasowitz, Abby S. 2000. *Using the Big6 to Teach and Learn with the Internet.* 1st ed. Worthington, OH: Linworth Publishing.

Klemm, William R. 2001. "Creating Online Courses: A Step-by-Step Guide." *Commentary.* May/June. Available at http://ts.mivu.org/default.asp?show=article&id=861 (accessed January 16, 2005).

Landau, Valerie. 2001. *Developing an Effective Online Course.* Seaside, CA: Round World Media.

Lynch, Marguerita M. 2001. *The Online Educator.* 1st ed. New York: Routledge Falmer.

Nickols, Fred. 2000. *The Goals Grid: A Tool for Clarifying Goals and Objectives.* Available at http://home.att.net/~nickols/goals_grid.htm (accessed January 13, 2005).

Porter, Lynnette R. 1997. *Creating the Virtual Classroom.* 1st ed. New York: Wiley Computer Publishing.

Porter, Lynnette R. 2002. *Developing an Online Curriculum: Technologies and Techniques.* 1st ed. Hershey, PA: Information Science Publishing.

Williams, Priya. 2003. "How to Develop an Online Course." *Online Course Development Tutorial and Process Checklist.* Available at http://stylusinc.com/online_course/tutorial/process.htm (accessed January 16, 2005).

Wolfe, Christopher R. 2004. *Learning and Teaching on the World Wide Web.* 1st ed. Hershey, PA: Information Science Publishing.

PERMISSIONS SUMMARY

The Nine Information Literacy Standards for Student Learning, excerpted from Chapter 2, "Information Literacy Standards for Student Learning," of *Information Power: Building Partnerships for Learning by American Association of School Librarians and Association for Educational Communications and Technology*. Copyright © 1998 American Library Association and Association for Educational Communications and Technology. Reprinted by permission of the American Library Association.

Notesheet for Checking Out a Course Site, from *Developing an Online Curriculum* by Leanette R. Porter (pp. 279-284), Copyright 2004 Idea Group Inc., www.idea-group.com. Reprinted by permission.

The Big6™ Skills reprinted with permission. Big6™ copyright © 1987 by Michael B. Eisenberg and Robert E. Berkowitz.

Excerpts from **The Goals Grid: A Tool for Clarifying Goals and Objectives** by Fred Nickols, reprinted with permission. Copyright © 2000 by Fred Nickols.

Rubric for Evaluating Behavioral Objectives, from *Developing an Effective Online Course* by Valerie Landau (Round World Media, 2001), reprinted with permission. Copyright © 2001 by Valerie Landau.

INDEX

ABOUT THE AUTHORS

PAMELA S. BACON is a full-time librarian and part-time author. For five years she has worked as the media center director at Ben Davis High School. During that time, she designed and implemented the "Capture the Giant" online orientation. She is also the author of *100 Library Lifesavers* and *100 More Library Lifesavers,* published by Libraries Unlimited.

DAVID BAGWELL JR. is the former technology supervisor at Ben Davis High School and the headmaster of the Indiana Online Academy. He currently teaches an online course at IUPUI focusing on research in educational technology.